❧ EARLY 3 Rs ❧

How to Lead Beginners Into Reading, Writing, and Arithme-TALK

❧ EARLY 3 Rs ❧

How to Lead Beginners Into Reading, Writing, and Arithme-TALK

Lee Mountain
University of Houston

LEA LAWRENCE ERLBAUM ASSOCIATES, PUBLISHERS
2000   Mahwah, New Jersey   London

Lawrence Erlbaum Associates, Inc., Publishers
10 Industrial Avenue
Mahwah, New Jersey 07430-2262

Cover design by Kathryn Houghtaling Lacey

Library of Congress Cataloging-in-Publication Data

Mountain, Lee Harrison
    Early 3 Rs : how to lead beginners into reading, writing, and
arithme-talk / by Lee Mountain.
        p. cm.
    Includes bibliographical references (p.)and index.
    ISBN 0-8058-3400-1 (pbk. : alk. paper)
        1. Early childhood education. 2. Language arts
(Early childhood). I. Title.
LB1139.23.M68 1999
372.21—dc21   99-38043
                                                            CIP

Books published by Lawrence Erlbaum Associates are printed
on acid-free paper, and their bindings are chosen for strength
and durability

Printed in the United States of America
10 9 8 7 6 5 4 3 2 1

To my wonderful grandchildren

◆ ◆ ◆

Contents

UNIT II: HOW TO HELP EARLY LEARNERS TAKE THEIR FIRST STEPS INTO THE 3 Rs

UNIT III: HOW TO EXPAND AND VARY STRATEGIES FOR EARLY TEACHING OF THE 3 Rs

UNIT IV: HOW TO SMOOTH THE TRANSITION INTO 3 Rs IN THE PRIMARY GRADES

◆ ◆ ◆

Preface

Maybe you want to become a teacher of young children, so you are taking coursework to learn about early instruction in reading, writing, and arithmetic. Or maybe you are already a teacher in a nursery school, child-care center, preschool program, kindergarten, or primary classroom.

Maybe you are a parent or grandparent of a preschooler and you want to give your child a strong homestart on reading, writing, and arithmetic.

Maybe you are an administrator building a developmentally appropriate academic program for early learners.

There is no "maybe," however, about one thing. There is one thing you know for sure: You know that an adult who values reading, writing, and arithmetic can give a young child an early start on the 3 Rs. So you want specific how-to-do-it procedures for promoting the emergence of literacy. Probably you are asking, "What can I SAY and DO to give each child (from a bright baby to an at-risk beginner) the best possible start on the 3 Rs?"

The purpose of this book is to answer that question. *EARLY 3 Rs: How to Lead Beginners Into Reading, Writing, and Arithme-TALK* provides easy-to-follow instructions for promoting emergent literacy and then for teaching the 3 Rs from preschool into the primary grades. With the strategies in this reader-friendly book, you can give personalized direct instruction to beginners in just a few minutes a day.

The progression of content extends from early preparation for the 3 Rs to enrichment of the basics in kindergarten and the primary grades. The instructional strategies begin with the oral approach (from phonemic awareness to *arithme-talk*) and then move on to print that is personally meaningful to a young child.

The chapters in Unit I explain how to foster a young child's growth toward reading, writing, and arithmetic. Unit II gives procedures for helping a beginner take the first steps into the 3 Rs. Unit III offers strategies for expanding and varying your early teaching of reading, writing, and arithmetic. Unit IV suggests ways to smooth the transition into the primary grades for early learners.

Students in early childhood education and literacy courses can learn with ease from this book. It is informal in style, practical in content, and suitable for all audiences who need a guidebook for teaching reading, writing, and arithmetic to early learners.

The distinctive features of this book include the following:

1. Integration of all *three* Rs—reading, writing, *and arithmetic*. Many books on early childhood education point out connections between reading and writing, but very few directly develop the arithmetic connection. Because arithmetic is language-based, it is treated herein as a component of early literacy.
2. Individualized techniques for direct teaching. Direct teaching of phonemic awareness, phonics, and word and number recognition is on the rise in early childhood education. This book offers specific strategies for personalized direct teaching of the 3 Rs to young children as they emerge into literacy.
3. Specific how-to-do-it instructions for using the oral approach. The chapters supply script after script of exactly what the teacher could say to pupils to promote their early learning of reading, writing, and arithmetic.

The structure of the book makes it easy to use. The pedagogical features include **unit previews, overviews,** and **unit summaries.** The preview for each unit explains what to do and why to do it. Each chapter opens with an overview, showing the topics featured in that chapter. Each unit concludes with a summary. At the end **(For Further Reading)** you will find a reference list of books related to early learning of the 3 Rs.

In many of today's field-based education courses, a student is required to initiate literacy instruction by working one-on-one with a young child. The personalized, oral approach in this volume gives the student the strategies needed to promote a beginner's emergent literacy and to offer direct instruction in the 3 Rs.

Early childhood educators often attend workshops and inservice training sessions to learn more about offering instruction in the 3 Rs to beginners. This book is an effective guide for them to follow as they put their learning into practice with their pupils.

ACKNOWLEDGMENTS

Many educators influenced my thinking as I wrote this book. I am most grateful to Dr. Terri Beeler, Dr. Sharon Crawley, Dr. Jennifer Moon, Linda Mountain, Naomi Silverman, and Nadine Simms. They would agree that it's a joy to lead young children into the early learning of reading, writing, and arithmetic.

Happy teaching!

Unit I

◆ ◆ ◆

HOW TO FOSTER GROWTH TOWARD READING, WRITING, AND ARITHMETIC

1

◆ ◆ ◆

Preview of Unit I:
Fostering Growth
Toward the 3 Rs

It is never too soon to start reading aloud to a child. In child-care centers and preschools, read-aloud time is part of the daily schedule. But even during midnight feedings of infants, the seeds of literacy can be sown.

"I'll get our nursery rhyme book," one mother told her baby, "as soon as I finish writing this note to your grandma. Then we'll cuddle in the rocking chair, and I'll read to you." This baby was born into a reading and writing environment. Even arithmetic received early attention in this baby's home because the mother frequently opened the nursery rhyme book to a toe-play counting chant, and read:

> The first little piggie went to market,
> The second little piggie stayed home,
> The third little piggie had roast beef,
> The fourth little piggie had none,
> The fifth little piggie cried "Wee, wee, wee,"
> All the way home.

At the end of the chant she said, "One, two, three, four, five," touching each of the baby's toes in turn as she counted. Obviously, in the nursery, she was not trying to teach her infant to count, any more than she was trying to teach the baby to read and write as she talked about her own reading and writing. But this mother was consciously using words connected with the 3 Rs. She was making sure the vocabulary of reading, writing, and arithmetic was a part of her baby's earliest language environment.

She knew in her heart what recent research has verified: by talking to her infant, she was making a real contribution to the growth of her baby's brain. Thanks to positron-emission tomography (PET) scans, researchers can now detect the activity in a baby's brain when the child is stimulated by speech. So the oral approach to early instruction has gained firm scientific support.

A child from a highly verbal home environment is likely to thrive on an early start on reading, writing, and arithmetic. But what about the children who come to you without having had the advantage of early verbal stimulation?

WHAT TO DO

You can help those children because you realize it is never too soon, even in a baby-care center or a nursery school, to immerse a child in the literate vocabulary of reading, writing, and arithmetic. And it is never too late, even in an elementary school remedial program, to recreate for a child the environment of a literate home.

You will make a major impact if you simply talk with your children, using language connected with reading, writing, and arithmetic, and get the children to respond in kind. Your contribution to their emergent literacy will be even greater if you involve them in the 3 Rs, and get them to talk to you in the vocabulary of the 3 Rs.

The preschool population is composed of a wide variety of children, some from highly literate homes, but others from homes that provide very little exposure to reading, writing, or arithmetic. The backgrounds of these children may have given them adequate vocabularies for talking about food, clothes, and daily activities. But most of them need more exposure to the oral and written language of the 3 Rs. You can provide what they need and thereby prepare them to learn reading, writing, and arithmetic.

The chapters in this opening section will give you specific how-to procedures for helping young children in the following ways:

- Immerse them in the oral language of the 3 Rs
- Speak "arithme-talk" to develop concepts
- Read aloud to them, with participation extras
- Get them ready for phonics—orally
- Surround them with written language, and talk about print
- Demonstrate writing, and talk about whatever they write
- Seize the teachable moment

These procedures are developmentally appropriate for young children. They foster growth toward literacy in many of the ways suggested by the National Association for the Education of Young Children and the International Reading Association. They lead toward early learning of the 3 Rs.

Although arithme-talk is featured in chapter 3 and environmental print in chapter 6, you want to address both simultaneously with your child. There is no chronological order for the activities in Unit I. All of them are of benefit to your child every day, and the more of them you can squeeze in every day, the better.

Your early learner might start the day by pretending to write an order from a fast-food menu and pay with play money at the cash register. In the next hour, you might play a phonemic awareness game with the child, read a counting book aloud, and help the child print his or her name. During all of these activities you are immersing the child in the language of the 3 Rs and promoting growth toward reading, writing and arithmetic.

WHY TO DO IT

From birth to age 6 is a magic time for language learning. In a language-immersion environment young children easily learn the vocabulary to which they are exposed. They need to hear the 3 Rs vocabulary from you as you constantly talk about reading, writing, and arithmetic.

Experts disagree about exact numbers as they try to keep track of the growth of a young child's speaking vocabulary, but they agree that it grows very rapidly. The pace represented by these "ballpark figures" would not be considered unusual:

Age	Approximate number of words
15 months	5
18 months	20
2 years	250
3 years	900
4 years	1,500
5 years	2,100
6 years	2,600

Of course, 6-year-olds who have a speaking vocabulary of 2,600 words may well have a listening vocabulary of 26,000 words or more, that they can comprehend. The figures, inexact as they may be, show the potential.

Teachers and parents who talk with their children build on that potential. There is a wide disparity in vocabulary size between toddlers with chatty mothers and toddlers with less talkative mothers. The number of times a child hears particular words is of special importance. Lots of repetition is beneficial. Young children begin to use the words they hear repeatedly.

Therefore, as you repeatedly use words connected with reading, writing, and arithmetic around your pupils, you have good reason to expect that they will come to comprehend, internalize, and use the vocabulary of the 3 Rs themselves. During the early years of rapid language development, a child can move comfortably from listening and speaking into reading and writing, and—because arithmetic is language-based—into the early learning of arithmetic, also.

Older theories of readiness for the 3 Rs have evolved into today's understanding of emergent literacy. Every child is ready to learn something that leads toward reading, writing, and arithmetic. There is not a sharp dividing line between the states of *not ready* and *ready*. Instead, there is a continuum of emergence into literacy, a progression of learnings that leads toward the 3 Rs.

Adults have always referred to a child's earliest attempts at speech as "talking." When a baby first says "Mama," the proud mother will tell you, "She's starting to talk." Two and three word utterances are welcomed with enthusiasm: "She's talking in sentences." Nobody expects a child to leap from babbling into full verbal command of our language. Speech develops in stages.

So does reading. So does writing. So does arithmetic. But adults are more hesitant about calling the early stages of literacy *reading, writing,* and *arithmetic*. A child's early attempts at written communication are often termed *scribbles*. However, to the child who solemnly hands you a birthday card she has signed, those scribbles are her name. In fact, she will "read" her name to you from the card.

If you ask a 4-year-old child how old she is, she may hold up the correct number of fingers, even if she has not yet mastered the one-to-one correspondence of counting. But she's made a start. She is on her way toward arithmetic. She is emerging.

So, as a teacher, you probably refer to a child's emergent-literacy behaviors as the beginnings of reading and writing and arithmetic. Your oral language activities will familiarize your children with the vocabulary and concepts of reading, writing, and arithmetic. This familiarity promotes emergent literacy and fosters growth toward the 3 Rs.

You are a literacy model for your students, constantly demonstrating literacy behaviors that the children can imitate. A good start on reading, writing, and arithmetic is the most valuable academic gift you can give to a young child. On with the giving!

2

◆ ◆ ◆

Immerse Children in the Oral Language of the 3 Rs

Overview

These are the topics you will meet in this chapter:

- Opportunities to Use the Language of the 3 Rs
- How to Talk About Writing
- How to Talk About Arithmetic
- How to Talk About Reading
- Interrelation of the 3 Rs Vocabularies
- You As a Language Model

OPPORTUNITIES TO USE
THE LANGUAGE OF THE 3 Rs

From the very first day that a child arrives in your classroom, you can start immersing him or her in the oral language of reading, writing, and arithmetic. To foster emergent literacy, you can easily and naturally use words that are connected with the 3 Rs, as you explain many of the things you do. When taking your first-day measurement of a child's height, for example, you might say:

I'm going to make a mark on the wall for your height.
Then, I'll measure from the floor to see how tall you are.
I can read the number from my tape measure, and
write it on this page of my record book.

Although you are speaking mainly about height, which is related to arithmetic, you are also showing the child how you use reading and writing, as you talk along about recording the number. Whenever possible, you want to intertwine the 3 Rs so your children understand their connections.

Often, when you show a child a new item that has to be assembled, you can demonstrate the reading of directions. Everything from a balance scale to a computer comes with assembly instructions. When you read the directions aloud, you can involve a child in helping you by saying:

> *This is the instruction sheet that tells us how to put*
> *all these pieces together. I'll read the directions to you.*
> *"Step 1: Put the base on the table." Let's find the base.*
> *Then you can put it on the table.*

How to Talk About Writing

Long before you expect a child to form a letter or print a word, you can draw the child's attention to the purposes and benefits of writing. Each time you put pencil to paper, you can say what and why you are writing. Sometimes you can weave in the vocabulary of reading and arithmetic too, as in this example of calendar talk:

> *Every day you see me print some book titles by*
> *the number for the date on the calendar. That*
> *writing helps me remember which stories I've*
> *read to you.*

Occasionally, you may want to spell a word orally as you print each letter. Long before a child knows the whole alphabet, the child may learn the spelling of his or her own name. If you had a student named Peter, and you had read stories about Peter Rabbit to your class, you could say:

> *Today I'm going to write "Peter Rabbit" on our*
> *calendar: P - e - t - e - r R - a - b - b - i - t.*
> *Peter Rabbit's name has the same letters in it*
> *as Peter Smith's name. See: P - e - t - e - r.*

You can talk about what you are saying in print whenever you write notes, make lists, label items, sign forms, number pages, take dictation from a child, or write instructions. Then you can read back what you have written to show the reading–writing connection. As you talk about the numbers, letters, words, and sentences you're writing, you are again using the vocabulary of the 3 Rs.

How to Talk About Arithmetic

Some routine activities lend themselves to 3 Rs language. Let's listen, as a classroom aide helps a child get ready to go outdoors.

I'll button the top button of the jacket for you.
That's the first button, button number one.
The next button down is the middle button.
That's the second button, button number two.
And the third button is button number three.
There, you're all buttoned up now.

That's *arithme-talk*, spoken as well as any parent or teacher could speak it. The speaker does not expect that the child will instantly learn to count because of that talk. It's just the background patter that immerses the child in the vocabulary of arithmetic by using words like *first, second, third, one, two, three, top, middle, next,* and *down*.

How to Talk About Reading

Every time you read aloud, it's easy to use the language of the 3 Rs. For example, when a child asks you to read Joseph Jacobs' old classic, *Jack and the Beanstalk*, for the third time, you might pick up the book and say:

We've read this book twice before,
so I know that you love the story.
Here's the title, "Jack and the Beanstalk,"
on the cover, and here's a picture of Jack.
The name of the author who wrote this
book is Joseph Jacobs. Now let's turn to
the first page, and I'll start reading to you.

In those few sentences, you used the words *read, book, twice, story, title, cover, picture, author, first,* and *page*. That's talking the talk of the 3 Rs. Since reading is the first R, the majority of those words are connected more closely to reading than to writing or arithmetic.

INTERRELATION OF THE 3 Rs VOCABULARIES

For young children, however, all vocabulary is interrelated. Words like *author* and *wrote* apply to both writing and reading. Words like *twice* and *first* apply not only to arithmetic but also to reading, writing, and everything else. So your 3 Rs talking helps the child with all early learning.

There is an easy way to blend a bit more arithme-talk into read-aloud time. Just talk about the age of the book. For a hot-off-the-press book, you might glance at the copyright date and say:

> *This book was published last year.*
> *It's only one year old.*

For an older book, which has remained popular for at least one generation, this statement might do:

> *I first heard this story when I was*
> *your age. My teacher read it to me.*
> *That was more than 15 years ago.*

Of course, "more than 15 (or 20 or 30) years ago" has no specific meaning to a young child. It does, however, suggest a long time rather than a short time. Your saying it is simply part of your constant effort to immerse your listeners in the vocabulary of arithmetic, as well as reading and writing.

When you introduce a classic folktale like *Cinderella* or *Beauty and the Beast*, you could say:

> *Your grandparents might know this story.*
> *It was being told even before they were*
> *born. Next time you see them, tell them the*
> *story, and see if they remember hearing it*
> *when they were little.*

Later in your children's education, they learn the ancient multicultural roots of folktales. But even as preschoolers, they can apply to stories the concepts of "one year old" or "many years old," "long ago" or "recently," if you point the way.

YOU AS A LANGUAGE MODEL

Children pick up language by imitating the adults who are their language models. As one of those adults, you are a tremendously important model. Your talking will have a cumulative effect on your early learners since you are helping their brains build the neural circuitry that enables them to learn more words later on. Speaking one-on-one with each child is most beneficial, but early learners also benefit from listening in groups.

Young children need to hear new words frequently before they will use the words themselves. But they are not likely to hear words connected with reading, writing, and arithmetic in home conversations as often as they hear words connected with meals, toys, and behavior. You can provide frequent exposures to the vocabulary of the 3 Rs, the vocabulary that they need as preparation for elementary school.

If you immerse a young child in the oral language of the 3 Rs, the words will gradually seep into the child's consciousness. Thanks to you, your students will hear the words frequently, understand them in context, respond to them, and eventually use them. This oral-language immersion is the first step in preparing young children for reading, writing, and arithmetic.

3

◆　◆　◆

Speak Arithme-Talk
to Develop Concepts

Overview

These are the topics you will meet in this chapter:

• Early Concept Development
• Arithme-talk About Weight
• Concepts Interrelated With Reading and Writing
• Matching, Categorizing, and Sorting
• The Vocabulary of Size
• Counting All Day

EARLY CONCEPT DEVELOPMENT

Most people think counting is the first concept that teachers address with children in early arithmetic. But you know it's not. You know that before children can count, they need to hear and use arithme-talk about concepts of quantity, such as size, measurement, and amount. You have heard young children talk about:

- *size*, in terms of "big" and "little"
- *measurement*, in terms of "a spoonful of sugar" and "a glass of milk"
- *amount*, in terms of "more" and "all gone"

Most toddlers pick up these concepts in the normal course of daily activities, like eating, sleeping, bathing, dressing, and playing. Many parents automatically say such things as "More?" and "All gone" to their toddlers at mealtime. But they don't automatically use words connected with a lot of other math concepts. So you need to speak arithme-talk regularly to help your pupils develop understanding of the concepts they need.

Let's consider how the concept-development process works, first in a non-mathematical area, and then in a mathematical area. Toddlers begin to understand the non-mathematical concepts of wet and dry while they're still in diapers, because they hear the words frequently. Eventually they can feel the difference between wet and dry. After they are beyond diapers, they still hear the words at bath time, and they start using them in their own speech.

The concepts of wet and dry are expanded further when the children get wet in the rain, when they go swimming, or when they dry dishes. These concepts get plenty of reinforcement, through both language and experience.

When you work on concepts associated with reading, writing, and especially arithmetic, you want to use the same type of approach that led to a child's mastery of the concepts of wet and dry, employing both language and experience.

ARITHME-TALK ABOUT WEIGHT

Sometimes you get unexpected bonuses, as you'll see from this story told by an arithme-talking preschool teacher.

> When I began talking to my girls and boys about the concept of weight, I weighed each child on my scale. Then I picked up a big box of blocks, weighed it on the same scale and said, "This box is heavy, but it's not as heavy as you. When I pick up this box, and then pick up one of you, I can feel that you are heavier. The box does not weigh as much as you weigh." Every day, I would manage to create a few minutes of conversation related to weight, saying things like: "How much does your new baby sister weigh? Oh, you weigh a lot more than she weighs."
>
> Once I brought in some groceries and said, "Hold the grapefruit in one hand and the orange in the other. Which feels heavier? Yes, the grapefruit does feel heavier. The orange is lighter than the grapefruit."
>
> "Who has seen your mother weigh oranges at the grocery store? Does the grocery scale look like the scale that I use to weigh you? No? What does it look like?"
>
> After about a week of such arithme-talk, I brought a balance scale to class to help me explain more about heavier and lighter. I showed the children that an apple was heavier than a bag of popcorn, and a big ball of cotton was lighter than a little rubber ball. Then I left the balance scale on a table so that any child who was interested could experiment with it.
>
> A child named Sierra, who had paid scant attention to my talk about heavier and lighter, discovered that she could make the two sides of the scale balance by putting a crayon on each side. After that discovery, balancing was the only thing Sierra wanted to do with the scale.

So, I got an unexpected bonus. Sierra leapfrogged the concepts of heavier and lighter and reached the more advanced concept of equal. I seized the teachable moment, followed Sierra's lead, and talked with her about the weights being equal, rather than pushing the concepts of heavier and lighter.

CONCEPTS INTERRELATED
WITH READING AND WRITING

Often, as in the story told by Sierra's teacher, one concept leads to another, and they all help in varying degrees with the early learning of arithmetic. But they are interrelated with reading and writing, so they also promote the emergence of literacy. There is a lot of overlap.

The concept of equal, for example, seems to belong mainly to the vocabulary of arithmetic. However, equal is also related to (but not synonymous with) same. And the concepts of same and different are useful in learning all 3 Rs—and everything else too.

To grasp the concepts of same and different, your children need a lot of background experience with activities that involve matching, categorizing, and sorting. These activities are continued and expanded in the primary arithmetic program.

Matching, Categorizing, and Sorting

You can start to involve children in matching activities when they are very young. To help them develop categorizing concepts, you can give them directions to sort familiar items, such as:

- *Put the crackers on this plate and the cupcakes on that plate.*
- *Stack the big blocks here and the little blocks there.*
- *Put the books on the shelf labeled "Books," and the dolls in the box labeled "Dolls."*
- *Sort the plastic farm animals, putting all the cows in the barn, the sheep in the field, and the horses in the stables.*
- *Match the socks (or mittens, napkins, cups, plates) by color or size.*

You might also have them sort by shape, putting circles in one pile and triangles in another, if they have grasped the same and different aspects of these shapes.

If not, maybe you could have them happily eat their way into the concepts of circle and triangle. The snack-time possibilities for circles include donuts, banana slices, vanilla wafers, and bagels. For triangles, a tasty approach might include tortilla chips, sandwiches cut diagonally, and fruit wedges.

The Vocabulary of Size

Some children become skillful at stacking and nesting at early ages. You may have a student who can stack 6 or more boxes in order of size, with the largest at the bottom and the smallest at the top. The same child may also be able to reverse the procedure and nest the boxes, putting the smallest inside the next smallest and proceeding right up to the largest. Stacking and nesting, however, are often performed in silence.

You want to promote arithme-talk about these procedures. Your children need to understand and use the vocabulary of size. As you admire a tall stack, you might say to the builder:

> *Where did you put the biggest box?*
> *Where is the smallest box?*
> *Which is taller—your stack or the table?*
> *Which is shorter—your stack or the bookshelf?*

Many children will point, rather than speak, to answer your questions. Correct pointing does show understanding of the concepts of biggest, smallest, taller, and shorter. But you want to lead the child to use the vocabulary of size. You may elicit a bit of that vocabulary if you say:

> *I'd like to build a stack like yours.*
> *Will you tell me how?*
> *What should I do to start?*

Even after this nudge, the child will probably be more inclined to show you than to tell you. And even if you succeed in getting the child to verbalize the process, the explanation may not include the size-words you are anticipating. A child who has learned colors, for example, might say about a three-block stack, "I put the yellow block on the red block, and the little blue block on top."

Then it's time for you to model what you hope you will eventually hear. Your arithme-talk about size might sound like this:

> *Yes, I see the smallest block on top*
> *and the biggest block at the bottom.*
> *Which block is in the middle?*

(If the child points correctly, continue.)

> *Yes, that's the middle block. It's bigger than*
> *the block on top. But it's smaller than the*
> *block on the bottom.*

One observant teacher noticed a pair of twins, Brooke and Crystal, playing interestingly with the stacking boxes. Brooke started building a stack. She placed the largest box face down on the floor, and the next-to-largest on top of it.

Crystal added another box to the stack, in the correct order of size. Then she stood back, apparently aware that it was her sister's turn.

But Brooke could not immediately find the box that was the right size to be stacked next.

Crystal did not join her sister in the hunt. Instead, while Brooke was still searching, Crystal located the box that she herself would add when it was her turn again. Then she stood back and waited her turn.

When Brooke found the right box and placed it on the stack, Crystal was ready to make the next addition immediately. But the stack was getting tall. She took some time to place her box on top very carefully.

And while she was being so careful, Brooke glanced once at the box her twin sister was holding, spotted the next two boxes that should be added in order of size, picked them up, and waited for Crystal to finish.

Not only were they taking turns, but they also seemed to be thinking ahead. They were stacking in silence, but the teacher gave words to what she saw happening:

> *Good for you, taking turns so well!*
> *And it's good, too, to think ahead about*
> *where each box belongs in your stack.*
> *Crystal, while your sister was hunting,*
> *you held the next box you would add.*
> *And, Brooke, you spotted two boxes*
> *in order of size that belong near the top.*

That teacher modeled how to talk about stacking. Brooke and Crystal just went on playing, but they heard the teacher's words about what they were doing. They could begin to absorb her vocabulary of size.

Your children need to hear and absorb your vocabulary of size, weight, time, distance, and measurement as you immerse them in your arithme-talk. Eventually they will internalize and use those vocabularies themselves.

COUNTING ALL DAY

Size, quantity, and shape concepts are important precursors of counting. But while your children are still mastering these background concepts, you can start building their familiarity with the 1, 2, 3s by immersing them in the arithme-talk of counting.

All through the day, it's easy to blend counting into the things you regularly do. For example, you probably have on display an attendance chart with each child's name on it, so that you can point to the names and read them, and write (making checkmarks) as you call the roll. To integrate arithmetic, you can count aloud. First, count the total number of pupils present. Then count just the girls, and after that, just the boys. Have some early arithme-talkers help you with the counting.

At snack time, you might have the children do the distributing:

Get just enough plates (napkins, spoons) for everyone at your table. And don't forget yourself.

That last sentence is especially important for young children, because their "miscounting" is often just a case of forgetting to count themselves.

At dessert time, you can provide more arithmetic activities by tabulating data and counting votes. As you write the words "vanilla" and "strawberry" on the board, you might ask, "What flavor of ice cream (or yogurt) do you like better, vanilla or strawberry?"

As each child answers in turn, you will write the child's name under either vanilla or strawberry. Then you can tell each child to stand up as you read his or her name, so that everyone can see "The Vanilla Group" and "The Strawberry Group." These groups might sit at separate tables for dessert. Then you can count their votes, write the numbers on the board, and talk about the numbers.

Many of the songs you sing with your children involve numbers and mathematical concepts. Consider the counting in "Ten Green Bottles" and "The Twelve Days of Christmas." If you use flannel board pictures to accompany those songs, you can make the counting concrete.

The song, "The Old Lady Who Swallowed the Fly," tracks creatures from the smallest to the largest. The verses of "The Farmer's in the Dell" proceed from largest to smallest. Such songs promote counting when you ask:

How many creatures did the old lady swallow? How many people were in the dell? How many animals were in the dell?

At clean-up time, you can promote counting and stacking, as well as neatness, by saying to a group:

Will each of you please pick up and stack three blocks, like this—1, 2, 3.

Demonstrate stacking as you say '1, 2, 3.'

Bring them to me, and I'll put them in the box.

Handing out slips for the children to take home can generate such counting questions as:

How many slips do we need for all of you?
How many just for the group at this table?

You can talk arithme-talk all day! And if you do, it will add to your immersion of your children in the oral language of the 3Rs and your promotion of their awareness of numbers.

4

◆ ◆ ◆

Read Aloud to Them, With Participation Extras

Overview

These are the topics you will meet in this chapter:

• Procedures for the First Read-Aloud of a Book
• Subsequent Rereadings
• Book Handling for Beginners
• Pupil Participation
• The Drama of a Read-Aloud Romp
• Comparing Different Versions of the Same Story
• Extras From Nonfiction Read-Alouds

PROCEDURES FOR THE FIRST READ-ALOUD OF A BOOK

All talk with young children is good; 3 Rs talk is better; and book talk is best of all. Book talk is what happens when you read aloud to your children, and they respond and participate.

Because young children love for you to read aloud to them, you probably include a read-aloud time in your schedule every day. Often your children just want to listen, and they definitely learn a lot from listening. With some books, however, they can learn even more by participating.

First, let's review the essentials that you cover, the basic read-aloud procedures you would use for any book. Then let's look at some extras you can add that will encourage children to participate more actively during read-aloud time.

Suppose you have a new book that you intend to read to your pupils. You want to call attention to the title, author, illustrator, age, and maybe awards of the book when you introduce it. You also want to encourage the children to make predictions about the story. So, for the first read-aloud of the book, you will probably say something like this:

> *This is a new book for our class.*
> *I've never read it aloud to you before.*
> *It won an award this year for the*
> *illustrations (show Caldecott Medal).*
> *Who can point to the title?*
> *Yes, the title is . . . (read the title aloud).*
> *There are some names on the cover of this*
> *book, the name of the author and the name*
> *of the illustrator (point to and read names).*
> *Let's look at the picture on the cover.*
> *That picture helps us know who we'll meet*
> *in this book. Who do you think we'll meet?*

Lead your children to base their predictions on the cover illustration. Most books for young children have art on the cover that corresponds to the art inside the book.

Subsequent Rereadings

On your second reading, your introduction probably moves faster through the basics. You and your children might discuss the accuracy of their initial predictions about the characters they would meet in the book. You might also ask what they remember about the story.

Consider how this procedure would work on the old folktale about the three little pigs and the big bad wolf. Before your first reading of *The Three Little Pigs* you would show your children the book cover, and ask what animals they expected to meet in the story. Someone would probably predict, "A wolf." Another pupil might say, "A pig." Before your second reading of the story, you would remind them of their guesses, and ask who had been right. Probably both children would say, "Me!"

"Yes, you were both right," you could reply. "We did meet a wolf in the story, and some pigs too. Do you remember what the pigs built?"

If you get the answer, "Houses," you'll want to ask, "How many?" Encourage your children to hold up three fingers and count on them, one, two, three.

You know that the pictures on the cover and inside the book will provide plenty of chances to work on counting. On each successive rereading of the story, you can draw out more of what each child remembers, not only about the cover and contents but also about each illustration. Soon the children will be chanting the refrains. Eventually, after a number of rereadings, you might have students try to retell the story in their own words.

As you reread favorite stories to your pupils, linger over the illustrations, page by page. Take time to draw out what your children remember, not only about the story but also about each illustration. Answer every question that a child raises, and ask some questions of your own. Also, try these extras that will encourage your pupils to participate more actively during read-aloud time.

BOOK HANDLING FOR BEGINNERS

The participation of some pupils may have to start with their physical act of turning the pages for you. Girls and boys who had no physical contact with children's books when they were toddlers may need help with holding a book right side up and opening it from the front, not the back. They need experiences with relatively indestructible cardboard, cloth, or even plastic bathtub books to develop their page-turning skills.

After these children learn to turn pages without tearing the paper, you can involve them with books that have movable tabs in the illustrations, and eventually even pop-up books. But your higher level aim is to lead them into verbal and mental, rather than just physical, participation at read-aloud time.

PUPIL PARTICIPATION

When you read a predictable story aloud, the big extra for your pupils is to join in, like a chorus. In *The Gingerbread Man,* for example, the hero's repeated taunt to his pursuers is:

> Run, run, run,
> As fast as you can.
> You can't catch me.
> I'm the gingerbread man.

After a few rereadings, the children can predict when that taunt is coming. Then you no longer need to read it. You can just hold up the book and point to those words, and the children in chorus supply the gingerbread man's chant.

Actually, they simply say the words from memory in all the right spots, but this type of memorization is a precursor of reading. It helps beginners make a connection between the words they hear and the words in print on the page. Predictable chorusing is a good extra for you to encourage at read-aloud time.

A similar type of extra is the chorusing that children do when they fill in a rhyming word for you at the end of a line. Suppose you were reading aloud from Dr. Seuss's *The Cat in the Hat*:

> And then something went BUMP!
> How that bump made us ____
>   (Pause for children to chorus "JUMP")

Given such clear context and illustrations in a book where the rhymes are very strong, some of your girls and boys will participate by coming up with the word *jump*, to rhyme with *bump*.

Sometimes children come up with non-rhyming words and chorus them too, when the context is very strong. In an *Old MacDonald* book, for example, they will quickly fill in the names of the animals and the sounds that the animals make.

THE DRAMA OF A READ-ALOUD ROMP

Another valuable extra is dramatizing. Your first step in dramatizing at read-aloud time is to change your voice for each character. The more extreme the changes, the better your children like it. For the Goldilocks story, for example, you need a wide range of pitches with a deep voice for Father bear and a high treble for Baby bear.

After you have demonstrated during a few oral readings how each character should sound, individual children may take the parts and give their dramatic renditions of the lines. Puppets, props, and costumes are additional extras that can promote even more dramatic participation during read-aloud time.

When a few of your children become enthusiastic about dramatic participation, story time can become a read-aloud romp. Consider how one teacher described the antics of two little girls, Patricia and Christine, and one little boy, Cliff, as she read *The Three Little Pigs*:

> I started by reading aloud the opening pages, telling how the three little pigs built their houses of straw, sticks, and bricks. Then I had the children help me line up three chairs for the three houses. I sat in the third (and largest) chair. Three of my pupils—Cliff, Patricia, and Christine—crowded around me because they wanted to claim roles in the story.
> Cliff said, "I'm the Big Bad Wolf."
> Patricia said, "I'm the first little pig."
> Christine said, "I'm the second."

I, as teacher, quickly claimed the role of the third little pig so that I could keep things under control.

Then Patricia and Christine took their places in their chairs, pretending that the first chair was the house of straw and the second chair was the house of sticks.

I held up the book so that they could see the words and pictures as I read to them about the approach of the Big Bad Wolf.

Cliff, pretending to be the Big Bad Wolf, jumped to his feet and strode right up to the first chair, the house of straw.

As I read, "Knock, knock, knock," Cliff pounded on the chair with his fist. Then he demanded, "Let me come in."

Patricia knew the answer by heart. She couldn't officially read it yet, but she was beginning to catch on to the print-speech connection. So I reached over to hold the page in front of her as I pointed to the words spoken by the first little pig. Patricia chanted them happily from memory: "Not by the hair of my chinny chin chin."

Cliff got red in the face, hyperventilating. "Then I'll huff and I'll puff and I'll blow your house down." He looked as if he were blowing out all the candles on his birthday cake. Then he wiped off his grin and growled in his best Big Bad Wolf voice, "Down goes the house of straw!"

Patricia hopped up on my lap, shrieking in delight.

Christine giggled and said, "Now me!" So we had a repeat performance in which she was the second little pig. When she heard, "Down goes the house of sticks," she jumped up to join Patricia on my lap.

Then we three were in the third house, the impregnable brick house. Christine glanced at the picture in our storybook: the Big Bad Wolf was approaching the door of the brick house. Patricia started to turn the page, and I whispered, "Not yet."

Cliff knocked on the back of my chair and shouted in his Big Bad Wolf voice, "Let me come in."

Christine and Patricia and I read our response in chorus. "Not by the hair of my chinnny chin chin."

When Cliff threatened once more to huff and puff and blow down the brick house, Patricia shouted, "No, you CAN'T."

Christine added, "We won't let you in, you Big Bad Wolf. You gotta come down the chimney."

They knew this story well.

I turned the page and read aloud, "Splash! The wolf fell into the big pot of water that was hanging in the fireplace. The little pigs wanted to cook him and eat him up. But he jumped out of the pot, then out of the window, then over the hedge. The three little pigs chased him until he was out of sight, and—" At that point read-aloud time turned into a romp with the girls chasing Cliff around the room.

Other folktales like *The Three Billy Goats Gruff* can lead to the same kind of dramatic read-aloud romp as *The Three Little Pigs*. The Bridge Troll, who threatens the three Billy Goats Gruff, is the same type of defeatable villain as the Big Bad Wolf. Little Billy Goat Gruff and Middle Billy Goat Gruff have similar lines. They both persuade the Troll to let them pass and to wait for Big Billy Goat Gruff, who tosses the Troll off the bridge. Many folktales lend themselves easily to dramatic participation at read-aloud time.

COMPARING DIFFERENT VERSIONS OF THE SAME STORY

Each author who retells a folktale puts his or her own twist on the tale. This fact is surprising to some early learners. When they come to know a folktale well, they will correct you if you deviate by even a word when you are rereading the familiar story aloud from the book that they have come to love.

But what if you bring in one or two or half a dozen other books that contain the same story? Well, almost the same story, since each author presents a slightly different version. Your children will be surprised and intrigued.

When you introduce a different version of a folktale from a new book, you open a world of opportunity for comparing and contrasting, not only the plot but also the illustrations. In the case of *The Three Little Pigs*, for example, any of these books would be a good follow-up for a read-aloud romp.

- Bishop, G. *The three little pigs*. Scholastic.
- Cauley, L. B. *The story of the three little pigs*. Putnam.
- Marshall, J. *The three little pigs*. Dial Books for Young Readers.
- Rounds, G. *Three little pigs and the big bad wolf*. Holiday House.
- Scieszka, J. *The true story of the three little pigs! by A. Wolf*. Viking Kestrel.
- Trivizas, E. *The three little wolves and the big bad pig*. McElderry Books.

The last two books in the preceding list are gentle parodies of *The Three Little Pigs*, in which even a wolf can be an appealing character. There are other versions of the folktale which you may find in the library closest to you. Any version beyond your initial read-aloud storybook will show that there is more than one way to tell the story. You need only two versions to take off on comparing and contrasting at read-aloud time.

EXTRAS FROM NONFICTION READ-ALOUDS

Some of the very best 3 Rs books have no story. They are alphabet books, counting books, concept books (colors, shapes, sizes, opposites), and informational books.

You often give direct instruction when you use these books at read-aloud time. They are excellent for combining the oral and written language of the 3 Rs, for integrating early reading, writing, and arithmetic, and for building 3 Rs concepts.

With counting books, for example, preschoolers can participate in counting the objects pictured on each page. You can have one child, then another, touch each object as you count, to emphasize the one-to-one correspondence.

With alphabet books, your students can name all the items on a page. You can then repeat the names—from the B page, for example: "Banana, ball, basket, bee." As you emphasize the /b/ sound at the beginning of each word, you are building your pupils' phonemic awareness.

You will find lists of counting books and alphabet books in later chapters of this book, along with suggestions on how to get the most instructional mileage from them.

With immersion in the oral language of the 3 Rs, lots of arithme-talk, and read-aloud times with participation extras, you are doing a wonderful job of fostering your children's growth toward reading, writing, and arithmetic.

5

♦ ♦ ♦

Get Them Ready
for Phonics—Orally

Overview

These are the topics you will meet in this chapter:

• Prior Knowledge About Sounds
• Attentive Listening
• Phonemic Awareness
• The Concept of "Word"
• Books that Feature Rhyming Words
• Auditory Discrimination
• Initial Sounds in Spoken Words

PRIOR KNOWLEDGE ABOUT SOUNDS

As background for phonics, talk about sounds with your children. Some of them will have learned animal sounds as toddlers. Others will be aware of sounds in terms of music, thunder, and alarm sirens. Yet, children need awareness of sounds in words (phonemic awareness) before they start to apply "sounding out words" to reading and writing. They will eventually need your focused and personalized teaching to learn the relationships between sounds and letters in print. But let's start with sounds only—the oral approach.

You can help your pupils activate their prior knowledge about sounds by asking such questions as:

— *What sound does the doctor tell you to make
when she looks down your throat?*

(Any child who has had experience with
the tongue depressor will answer "Ah.")

— *What sound do I make when I want you to be
quiet?* (Sh)
— *What sound do some people make about a good
meal?* (Mmm-mmm)

One teacher said that the hardest part of teaching about sounds was the
noise her pupils made in the classroom. She kept telling her pupils, "I want you
to be so quiet that you can hear a pin drop. Only then can you really listen for
sounds."

But even when the children stopped talking, closed their eyes, and listened
hard, it was not quiet enough to hear a pin drop. This teacher and her pupils
could then hear the drip of the water faucet, the hum of the heating system, and
the patter of rain against the window panes.

At that point, the teacher decided to take a different approach to "hearing a
pin drop." She stuck her straight pin back into her pin cushion and dropped a
bowling *pin* as the opener for her lesson on sounds.

ATTENTIVE LISTENING

Of course every teacher wants attentive listening from her pupils. As you immerse your pupils in the vocabulary of the 3 Rs, you know that they will gain
much more if they are listening attentively than if they are just hearing passively
(though even the passive hearing of 3 Rs vocabulary brings benefits to young
children).

Some teachers who want attentive listening ask for eye contact when they
are talking directly to one pupil. In kindergartens and nursery schools, you can
frequently hear a teacher say to a child:

*Look at me. What I'm going to say is important,
so keep looking at me. We can listen better
when we are looking straight at each other.*

Just as teachers want attentive listening from their pupils, so do the pupils
want attentive listening from their teachers. You can convey your interest to a
verbal child by maintaining eye contact while the child speaks and by responding appropriately.

Sometimes it is hard to respond appropriately because you can't quite understand what the child is saying. The simple statement, "Tell me again, please," certainly shows the child that you want to understand.

When you catch a few words but can't make out other words in a child's stream of speech, you can repeat the words you did understand and raise a question about the ones you did not catch:

> *You say that you went — where?*
> *I understood what you said about the*
> *merry-go-round. But I'm not sure I*
> *understood about the other ride. And*
> *I want to hear about it, so say it again.*

Your children enjoy feeling that you are hanging on their every word. Besides, your attention stimulates their speech development. The clearer their speech, the better chance they have of profiting from the oral approach to phonics via phonemic awareness.

PHONEMIC AWARENESS

There is a big difference between being aware of sounds in general and being aware of sounds within words. Very few children will have difficulty with a sound game that requires them to close their eyes and locate a buzzer in one corner of the classroom. At early ages they can match animals with their sounds ("mooo" for the cow, "meow" for the kitten). But those are much easier tasks than recognizing a speech sound (phoneme) at the beginning of a word.

In the flow of speech, children build awareness of the concept of *word* only if you call specific words to their attention. They absorb your vocabulary, and even come to use many of your words in context, but they often need a great deal of help in focusing on the sounds within a specific word.

The Concept of "Word"

For phonemic awareness, they need to form the concept of a *word* that they hear in the flow of speech. A preschooler might identify "no more" as one word, and "chickens" as two words. You can get your students to count words in short sentences by giving each of them blocks to use as counters.

Demonstrate with these sentences, placing a block in line (left to right) each time you say a word. Speak slowly.

> *Dogs bark.*
> *Joy can swim.*
> *Did you see Chang?*

After your children have seen you line up two, three, and four blocks as you spoke the words in these sentences, let them try. Some will catch on quickly. Those children will soon discard the blocks, and be able to count the words in your sentences on their fingers. Others will need lots of practice. For them, speak very slowly. For all your pupils, use one-syllable words in this word-counting game, since syllables may confuse the issue.

Your most capable early learners may already have started to grasp the concept of "word" as it applies to print. A child may be able to point to the word "milk" on milk cartons. But that same child may not be able to isolate a word in the flow of speech.

Books That Feature Rhyming Words

One of the easiest approaches to phonemic awareness is through rhyme. Read-aloud time is great for building your children's auditory sense of rhyme. They enjoy hearing verse, from nursery rhymes to children's poetry. As previously mentioned, you can lead them to participate in chorus at read-aloud time by encouraging them to supply a missing rhyme at the end of a line.

Any rhyming book can lend itself to this kind of participation by your students, but you might want to use some of these tried-and-true titles by authors who handle rhyme especially well.

- Chapman, C. *Pass the fritters, critters.* Four Winds Press.
- Guarino, D. *Is your mama a llama?* Scholastic.
- Hoberman, M. A. *A house is a house for me.* Puffin.
- Kuskin, K. *Roar and more.* Harper Trophy.
- Martin, B., & Archambault, J. *Chicka chicka boom boom.* Simon & Schuster.
- Oppenheim, J. *Not now! said the cow.* Bantam.
- Prelutsky, J. *Tyrannosaurus was a beast: dinosaur poems.* Greenwillow.
- Seuss, Dr. *One fish, two fish, red fish, blue fish.* Beginner Books.
- Silverstein, S. *A giraffe and a half.* HarperCollins.
- Zemach, M. *Hush, little baby.* E. P. Dutton.

Suppose you are reading aloud from a nursery rhyme book, and you repeatedly chant the old favorite, "Jack and Jill went up the hill," until your pupils are well acquainted with it. Then, when you pause to let them supply the word *hill* (to rhyme with *Jill*), good things happen. Some of them will chorus the word *hill*, and that will encourage others to join in.

If you have a boy named Bill in your class, you can stop and say, "The word *hill* rhymes with *Jill*, and so does the name *Bill*. Listen—*hill, Jill, Bill.* What other words rhyme with *hill* and *Jill* and *Bill*?"

Maybe a child will come up with *fill* or *pill*, or perhaps even a nonsense word like *vill*. If it rhymes, accept it. You're trying to help your children grasp the concept of rhyme, and *vill* does rhyme. You may honestly say, "Yes, I hear the rhyming sound at the end of 'vill,' but that's not a word that we hear and say."

AUDITORY DISCRIMINATION

A simple oral game can help you determine which children have enough auditory discrimination to notice differences between speech sounds. To prepare for the game, you could start with words (rather than speech sounds), saying:

> *Listen to the name I say as I hold up*
> *each finger. One will be different from*
> *the others: Harold, Harold, Rocky, Harold.*
> *Which one is different?*

Your children will probably identify Rocky as the different name with ease. All they need for the "name" version of the game is an understanding of the concepts of same and different. But it's a little harder with sounds:

> *Listen to the sound I make as I hold up*
> *each finger. One will be different from*
> *the others: /h/, /h/, /r/, /h/.*
> *Which one is different?*

Some of your children will probably repeat the sound /r/, or point to the finger you held up when you said /r/. You can play this game with many other pairs of sounds to develop your pupils' abilities to hear similarities and differences. They need plenty of experiences with sounds before they can identify sounds at the beginnings of words.

Initial Sounds in Spoken Words

The next step is to get your pupils listening for the sound at the beginning of a word. For words that start with the same sound, you might tell your children:

> *I'm going to say two words.*
> *Do they start with the same sound*
> *or with different sounds? ball, boy.*

If you emphasize the sound /b/ at the beginning of each word, some of your children will probably be able to figure out that they start with the same sound.

When you say two words that start with different sounds (for example, *ball* and *top*,) you would again emphasize the beginning sounds so that your pupils have a good chance of hearing the difference.

To go one step further with such oral games, you might try these possibilities with a child:

- *In the refrigerator I keep something to drink that starts with the sound /m/. What is it?*

   (milk)

- *I see two things in our classroom that begin with the sound /t/. What are they?*

   (table, toys)

- *Three foods you like to eat for dessert start with the sound /k/. What are they?*

   (cake, cookies, candy)

In these early stages of developing phonemic awareness, your pupils will probably need reminding that the word *milk* starts with the sound /m/, or that *table* starts with the sound /t/, or that *cake* starts with the sound /k/. By all means, give them as many reminders and clues as they need.

The important thing is that you're building their early awareness of spoken sounds *orally*. Only after a child has an oral/aural grasp of sounds in words (phonemic awareness) can the child progress into using phonics as a tool for reading.

Many young children stay at the oral stage for quite a while as they build familiarity with sounds in words. But if they develop phonemic awareness during their period of emergent literacy, they will do better when they try to apply phonics to words in print.

6

◆　◆　◆

Surround Them
With Written Language,
and Talk About Print

Overview

These are the topics you will meet in this chapter:

- Print in Literate Homes
- Environmental Print
- Equipment for Writing
- Numbers in Print
- Equipment for Measuring
- Reading in Comfort
- Favorites for Your Classroom Library
- Interacting With Print

PRINT IN LITERATE HOMES

Interior-design magazines may favor early American decorating for young children, but literate parents decorate with an eye to the child's academic future. These parents often buy crib mobiles that feature A, B, C, along with 1, 2, 3. The curtains and wallpaper in the nursery show pictures and words. Numbers and letters abound on baby clothes, blankets, even the changing table pad. The baby's date of birth, length, and weight appear on wall hangings, plaques, and stork ornaments.

These parents know it is never too soon to give a child a print-rich room. The children from such homes begin school well acquainted with print. They are ready to progress smoothly into reading, writing, and arithmetic.

But what about the child who comes to you with very little awareness of print. How can you help this child?

You can create a print-rich room by stocking your room with many different kinds of printed material, not only books to read but also old magazines and newspapers that your children can cut up. You want activity areas (or centers) in your room for interacting with print as it relates to reading, writing, and arithmetic.

Of course, you want letters and numbers everywhere—on flannel boards, blocks, wall charts, magnetic boards, games and picture cards. You want toys that feature print, such as telephones and cash registers. These items are basic, and they are often found in literate homes as well as classrooms.

ENVIRONMENTAL PRINT

You also want to surround your children with a form of print that is less frequently displayed in homes. It is the familiar environmental print that the children encounter when they look out the window of a car or bus, when they go to the grocery store, when they see ads on television. Even very young children are likely to have seen environmental print on:

- traffic signs (STOP, numbers on highway exits)
- product labels (on containers and wrappers)
- names of favorite places (toy stores, restaurants)
- cereal boxes (that show the names in big letters)
- advertisements that feature familiar logos
- print on banners and pennants

You can make sure that your children interact with that familiar print by identifying each item as you mount it for display and then referring to it frequently. You can say things like:

- *Line up in front of the STOP sign.*
- *Put the stuffed animals under the ZOO banner.*
- *Which cereal is your favorite? Find its name on one of our cereal boxes.*
- *Selina, Sylvester, Sam, and Salim all have names that start with S. Bring me a traffic sign that starts with the same letter.*

It takes time and effort to amass a good collection of environmental print, but parents are usually eager to help. One kindergarten teacher, who had great luck with parents, reported:

Once they caught on, there was no stopping them. The parents swamped me with environmental print. They brought fast-food menus, placemats, bumper stickers, theme park signs, posters and t-shirts of their favorite athletic teams, mottoes on wall plaques, and of course piles of print-rich boxes and containers from toy stores and grocery stores. I had enough environmental print to highlight a different item every day for months.

That teacher's one-item-a-day idea has merit. Although she graciously acknowledged every contribution, she still managed to avoid cluttering her classroom with too many displays. She was careful not to confuse or overwhelm her pupils.

All print is grist for your mill when you are creating a print-rich room, but you still need to chose carefully what pieces of environmental print to introduce, display, and review, to attract and retain the interest of your pupils.

Just as you don't expect children to understand every word they hear, you surely don't expect them to recognize and remember every word they see in your print-rich room. It's cause to celebrate when a child comes to know by sight even one or two of the words featured in your displays of environmental print.

EQUIPMENT FOR WRITING

Another element of a print-rich room is a writing center. Scribbling is an early stage of writing, so you want to provide your children with lots of opportunities to make a stab at written communication. They may start by making unintelligible scribbles. But then they may progress toward trying to print their names, send mail, and read aloud to you whatever they intended or pretended to write.

The basic writing equipment found in literate homes includes pens, pencils, erasers, and crayons. But in your print-rich writing center, you also want to supply as many other writing materials as possible, such as:

- paint and easel
- colored chalk and a chalkboard with erasers
- felt-tip markers of many sizes and colors
- finger paint
- paper of all sizes and colors
- stationery and envelopes
- index cards
- pads and notebooks
- sticky notes
- greeting cards

- carbon paper, tracing paper, and stencils
- magic slate
- pan of sand for finger writing
- sandpaper letters and numbers
- playdough to form into letters and numbers
- flannel board with letters and numbers
- mailbox

Your writing center can promote arithmetic as well as reading since, with your guidance, the children in your class can try to print the numerals in their addresses and phone numbers, soon after they start printing their names.

NUMBERS IN PRINT

Undoubtedly, the displays of environmental print in your print-rich room will feature more words than numbers. But numbers do appear in environmental print. Consider the outdoor speed limit signs, the numbers posted in tall print at filling stations for gas prices, and the address numbers on houses, stores, and curbs.

Children see numbers in print in their indoor environments too, on television channels, radios, microwaves, dials, and thermostats. But home conversations about such items are often limited to "Don't touch."

Your pupils encounter both letters and numbers on equipment ranging from blocks to computer keyboards. But probably the most common letters and numbers device is the telephone. If you have a telephone in your classroom, you might use it to integrate the "print" of arithmetic with reading and writing, by saying to a child:

I want to telephone your mother and tell her how well you painted today. Her telephone number is printed on her business card. I'll read it to you and show you each number, on the card and on the telephone. That way, you can help me call her.

In your print-rich room you can make good use of the environmental numbers that appear as prices on fast-food menus, tags in a store, and sale ads. You can call attention to the prices when children pay at the toy cash register for their favorite meals from the fast-food menus. This type of play promotes the emergence of numerical literacy (numeracy), since the children are noticing and responding to numbers in print.

EQUIPMENT FOR MEASURING

In a print-rich measuring center in your classroom, it is good to have plenty of equipment that your pupils can use for measuring length and width, height and depth, weight, temperature, time, cost, and quantity.

You and your pupils can use and talk about the numbers on the following measuring-center equipment:

- rulers
- measuring tapes
- yardsticks
- balance scales
- bathroom scale
- thermometers
- clocks
- timers (hourglass, egg timer, timer with buzzer)
- calendars
- play money
- cash register
- measuring cups
- measuring spoons
- containers for a half pint, a pint, a quart, a half gallon, a gallon, and for amounts in the metric system
- straws (or other manipulatives for counting and bunching)
- numbers (magnetic, felt, wooden, puzzle inlays)
- shapes (for matching and grouping circles, squares, and triangles)
- string, paper, blunt scissors, buckets, and sand (for measurement activities)

READING IN COMFORT

Perhaps the richest part of your print-rich room is the reading center. You want to make it as comfortable and inviting as possible with pillows, a rocking chair, a beanbag chair, good lighting, and some small rugs or carpet samples for children who want to lie on the floor to look at a book.

Of course, the more books, the better! And the more visible you can make the covers, the better. Low shelves are ideal for displaying picture books. You want your boys and girls to be able to find their favorites easily after read-aloud time.

Perhaps your school has an easel or stand for big books with their accompanying little books. Some kindergarten reading centers include an audiotape player and earphones for books with tapes. The pockets in shoe holders are handy for holding smaller books.

Favorites for Your Classroom Library

Garage sales, library sales, and secondhand bookstores can help you build your own classroom library without breaking your budget. Be sure to collect as many alphabet books and counting books as possible. A print-rich room is not complete without lots of books that feature a, b, c and 1, 2, 3.

Of course, you'll also want well-illustrated folktales and fairy tales in your permanent collection, too. Have as many versions as possible of these old favorites:

- Goldilocks and the Three Bears
- The Three Little Pigs and the Big Bad Wolf
- Little Red Riding Hood
- The Gingerbread Man
- The Three Billy Goats Gruff
- The Little Red Hen
- Jack and the Beanstalk
- Hansel and Gretel
- The Frog Prince
- Cinderella
- Snow White and the Seven Dwarfs
- Rumplestiltskin
- Rapunzel
- The Elves and the Shoemaker

Fables are forever popular with young children. They are brief, often are about animals, and are strong conveyors of important messages. You will want some books of fables in your permanent collection. These fables are particularly good for reading aloud:

- The Tortoise and the Hare
- The Boy Who Cried Wolf
- The Lion and the Mouse
- The Wolf in Sheep's Clothing
- The Goose that Laid Golden Eggs
- The Crow and the Pitcher

In addition to the old favorites, you need a constant succession of new titles for your reading center. Many libraries are generous in their lending policies for teachers, so you can probably keep your reading center's offerings fresh all year with a variety of appealing books.

INTERACTING WITH PRINT

All the books, environmental print, and equipment you can collect for your print-rich room, however, will do only a little to foster emergent literacy, unless you get your children to interact with the print. That print is not just decoration. It is the text from which they learn to identify words, to recognize a few, and perhaps to copy them and use them in their own written communication.

So, exactly what can you say and do to get the children interacting with the print? You might start with a simple matching activity:

> *Here's one wrapper for oatmeal cookies.*
> *See—it says "Oatmeal Cookies" in big print,*
> *two words, oatmeal and cookies, with a space*
> *between them. See the space.* (Point at it.)
> *I know we have two of these wrappers.*
> *Let's hunt through the pile and find the*
> *other one that says "oatmeal cookies."*

You worked on building the concept of "word" orally when you talked about individual words in the flow of speech. Now, with environmental print, you can point out the visible space between printed words. This helps your children start to form the concept of a "word" in print. They can begin to think of a printed "word" as letters close together with a space before and a space after.

Encourage them to carry this concept over into their writing. Early writers are inclined to run their words together, leaving little or no space between, even when they are copying.

You can further expand the concept of "word" as you talk about environmental print, along these lines:

> *I see the word flakes on all three of these cereal*
> *boxes—corn flakes, bran flakes, and frosted flakes.*

(Use your hands to frame the word flakes on each box.)

> *Now, who can frame the word flakes on this box*
> *just the way I did?*

An early writer might copy labels at the writing center, to make a grocery list. But some of your pupils may need an easier way to work with environmental print. With a different approach to making a grocery list, you can involve younger children.

Most people write grocery lists on paper.
But we're going to make a grocery list you
can carry in this big carton. Each of you will
name something you like, find its container
on our shelves, and put it in this carton.

Most traffic signs have distinctive shapes and use all capital letters. You can display them effectively as environmental print. They foster growth toward arithmetic (shapes) and writing (printing). Your children can interact with them when you say:

Let's use the big traffic signs on the wall
as our models when we make small traffic
signs to use with our toy cars. We want to
copy the shapes as well as the words.

"I spy" games can get players to notice the print on book covers as well as the print on signs and labels. Suppose you say:

I spy the word "soup" somewhere in our room.
Find it.

You may be looking at the label on a can of soup as you speak, but life is full of surprises. Perhaps a child will bring you the storybook, *Stone Soup*.

The children who participate in 3 Rs activities with the print in your room will learn from that print. It can be one of their best stepping stones toward reading, writing, and arithmetic.

7

◆　◆　◆

Demonstrate Writing, and Talk About Whatever They Write

Overview

These are the topics you will meet in this chapter:

• Home Background for Writing
• Reasons to Write in Class
• Praise for all Attempts
• More Help as Needed
• Writing Jobs to be Done
• Mail Call

HOME BACKGROUND FOR WRITING

Some parents keep a pencil and a pad beside the telephone. Some use a refrigerator magnet to hold up an ongoing grocery list. Some leave post-it notes stuck to the bathroom mirror. The children of those parents know that writing is purposeful, and they come to you eager to learn to write.

But some children have seen little or no writing done at home, so they don't understand the purpose of writing and they are not interested in trying to write. Or maybe they've heard that you have to be able to spell before you can write. Or maybe it's just that, with their immature motor skills, the best they can do is scribble. In each of these cases, you can do specific things to help that are developmentally appropriate for each beginner.

REASONS TO WRITE IN CLASS

Every time you write anything, you can call your children's attention to your purpose, your reason for writing:

– *I'll write down the date of your birthday,
Ashley, so I'll remember.*
– *Let's write a note to Stoney
about changing the time of the picnic.*
– *If your name is on the list that I wrote
on the board, I want you to come here.*
– *We want to thank the fire fighters who
visited our class, so we'll write to them.*

Suppose you ask your pupils to help you make a list of what is needed for a class party. As each child dictates an item, you can write it on the board, very purposefully. Then you and your children can read the list together, to make sure nothing has been left out. Finally, you can count and number the items on the list to see how many things you need to get for the party.

One list can show your pupils the usefulness of all 3 Rs, as you say:

*You told me what to write on the list.
We read it. Then we counted the items,
and wrote a number beside each one.
Reading, writing, and arithmetic are a
big help when you're planning a party.*

PRAISE FOR ALL ATTEMPTS

Many a beginner is happy to scrawl one squiggly line in the middle of a page, with no concern even for forming letters (not to mention spelling), and then tell you that she has written a story for you. The child may read this "writing" back to you. Of course, you want to welcome such efforts and talk about them, because they show that the child is grasping the writing-reading connection.

As you walk around your classroom, moving from scribblers, who are not even familiar with the alphabet, to inventive printers, who can form some capital letters, your commentary might sound like this:

*I see you wrote something under your painting,
Kevin. Will you read it to me, please?*

(He says that his marks mean
"Kevin painted this.")

You wrote something under your painting too,
Luanne. I see "by Luan."

("Yes," she answers, "but I need more
letters in my name, don't I?")

You definitely want to help Luanne with the spelling of her name since she is
asking you directly about the letters.

Of course, the time will come in elementary school when Luanne and all
your other pupils will need to use both capital and lower-case letters, as well as
standard capitalization, punctuation, and spelling, whenever they write. But
those skills are not critical for the earliest attempts at writing. The important
thing is to get your beginners to realize what they can do with written language.
Polishing toward total correctness comes later.

More Help As Needed

Even the children who are slow to develop fine motor skills can make a stab at
writing, if you show a willingness to read their attempts at printing and an interest in talking about what they have written.

For these children, you can promote writing *without* pencil and paper. Maybe
they can arrange sandpaper letters, pasta letters, or magnetic or felt letters for
their messages. Also, if a pencil is unwieldy and paper is too easily torn, why not
substitute a big thick piece of chalk and let them try to write on the pavement
outdoors? Drawing and painting may lead into writing for these girls and boys.
Sometimes, holding the pencil along with you, as you write or print, helps them
get the feel of writing.

Of course, you'll display as much of their writing as possible in your print-rich
room. Some children may want to copy a favorite sign from the environmental-print display, and have you hang it alongside the original. Some may try to
write stories for posting on the bulletin board.

A few may want to write numbers on the chalkboard to help you tally, count,
or keep score in a game. More will be interested in seeing you write (and maybe
they'll copy) the number in the date for their birthday.

But most of them will start as Kevin and Luanne did, simply by labeling their
drawings with their names. They may know from home that name-writing is important, because they may have signed their names on greeting cards and letters
that their parents have mailed.

Writing Jobs to be Done

Every day someone has to update the calendar sentence on the chalkboard. At
the beginning of the school year it is your job to change "Today is Tuesday, September 1" to "Today is Wednesday, September 2." But one of your children

might soon be ready to take on the job. With a little help from you, that child might form a recognizable "3" or "4." With more help (and model words to copy), the child might fill in the blank with the word *Thursday* or *Friday*.

In the same way, the classroom weather report needs daily updating. The weather keeps changing from sunny to cloudy to rainy, from warm to cool to cold. Writing a whole sentence is a daunting task for beginners. Your neatly printed words, "The weather is ____ ," can stay in place. But your early writers may be eager to add just one word, the word for the blank.

Early in the school year, you probably did all the printing of your children's names on the classroom helpers chart. As soon as possible, you will want to add to the chart a column entitled, "Job done." Then, after a child feeds the fish, counts the erasers, or hands out forms, that child can print his or her name on the helpers chart in the "Job done" space.

Mail Call

Featuring a mailbox in your print-rich room stimulates writing because everyone loves to receive mail. If you write a note a week to each of your children, some of them may try to write you back.

Of course, you want your notes to be quite short, starting "Dear (the child's name)" and ending "Love, (your name)" with only a brief message in between. You know best what you can write that will be meaningful to each child. But even when no personally meaningful message springs to your mind, you can still keep the mail flowing by writing such general purpose positive sentiments as:

> – *I am happy to see you every day.*
> – *You have a great smile.*
> – *I am glad you are in my class.*
> – *It is fun to hear you laugh.*

One teacher wrote this 3 Rs rhyme to a child:

> *A, B, C. 1, 2, 3.*
> *I like you. Do you like me?*

Among this teacher's early writers, there was one child who responded to the question in the rhyme by printing, "I love you." What a prize! It is emotionally delightful when your children show affection; it is professionally delightful when they show progress toward the 3 Rs.

Signals of progress may come when you least expect them. You need to be on the lookout every day so that you can grasp the teachable moment for helping each child take early steps into reading, writing, or arithmetic.

8

◆　◆　◆

Seize the Teachable Moment

Overview

These are the topics you will meet in this chapter:

- Differences Among Young Learners
- General Signs
- Subtle Signs
- Spotting the Moments
- Your Decisions

DIFFERENCES AMONG YOUNG LEARNERS

Some children start learning the 3 Rs at the age of five, four, or even three. Some have difficulty starting on reading, writing, and arithmetic even after they are 6, 7, or 8 years old. Some progress into reading sooner than writing or arithmetic. Some count with complete comprehension long before they read. So consider each child individually as you watch for the teachable moment.

General Signs

The general signs of early progress toward the 3 Rs are easy to spot. Just think of the behaviors you see in those children who seem to have been naturally verbal almost from birth. What do they do?

- talk about everything
- follow a series of oral directions
- memorize nursery rhymes, counting rhymes, songs, and stories
- understand and use the vocabulary of reading, writing, and arithmetic
- sit still for 3 Rs activities
- look at picture books on their own
- request specific books at read-aloud time
- retell familiar stories in their own words
- elect paper and pencil activities
- show manual dexterity with puzzles and toys
- grasp concepts of size, shape, color, and quantity
- attempt to print letters and numbers
- stay focused on an activity to completion

A child who shows these signs will probably have no difficulty in starting to learn reading, writing, and arithmetic at an early age.

Subtle Signs

Some signs are not so clear or obvious. Some may be rather subtle, as shown by this teacher's story about spotting a kindergartener's indication of catching on to an arithmetic concept:

> Raul heard very little English at home, so he needed more preparatory activities for reading and writing. But he showed an early interest in numbers. So I started showing him the one-to-one correspondence of counting, using different objects every day.
>
> On Monday, I counted aloud for him, as I put four pegs in four holes. For the next few days, we set the table together, putting out one, two, three plates, and then one, two, three cups, as we counted aloud together. After that, he and I counted finger puppets for Snow White's seven dwarfs, as I put the seven puppets on seven of his fingers.
>
> The next week, at recess, I took Raul and the other children outside to play. I decided to make a ring-toss game for them, so I stood three sticks up straight beside a pile of rope rings. Then I demonstrated how to play, standing quite close to the sticks and tossing a ring over each.
>
> I told Raul, "Now you try. Grab some rings and see if you can get them on these sticks."
>
> He grabbed four rings, and he tossed (dropped) the first ring on the first stick, the second ring on the second stick, and the third ring on the third stick.
>
> Then he just stood there, gazing at the ring he was still holding, the fourth ring. Raul looked at the sticks again. Then he looked at me with a puzzled expression. Finally, he just walked away.

Though he said nothing, I felt that I knew just what he was thinking. His expression said to me that something had registered about the one-to-one correspondence of counting. Three rings on three sticks—that was the way things were supposed to be. There was no fourth stick for the fourth ring, so he just walked away, still holding that fourth ring.

It was a subtle signal, true. Raul didn't verbalize a question. With his limited English proficiency, he couldn't. But I felt that his behavior was an indicator that I should work with him individually as soon as we went back inside. And I was right. He clicked on counting. It was the teachable moment.

From this teacher's story, you know that she could spot a signal when she saw one. Raul's signal would not be found on any traditional list. In his own way, however, Raul was saying, "Teach me now."

SPOTTING THE MOMENTS

No doubt, in your print-rich room, you have spotted some indicators that only you could see, because you know your pupils so well. Perhaps your children can now recognize some environmental-print labels on containers. Maybe their recognition is based as much on design or color or position as on letters. Yet, the children are still showing some capability to identify words in print and to discriminate between one word and another. So it may be time for you to offer these children more structured reading instruction.

At your writing center, has any child progressed from scribbling to printing capital letters that you can recognize? If so, it's probably time to teach that child to print more letters.

Are any of your children speaking arithme-talk about shapes or quantities? Are any (like Raul) speaking body language that shows their sense of the one-to-one correspondence in counting? Do they line up or sort items by size? Do they use the word *two* when speaking of eyes, ears, hands? Can they distribute crayons evenly at their tables?

If you keep your antennae up, you may spot signs of progress toward arithmetic that others would miss, because others don't know your children as well as you do.

Your Decisions

You are the best person to decide when a child should take the first steps into reading, writing, or arithmetic. The best way to teach a young child any new material is to use the easiest possible method for a few minutes a day of personalized one-on-one time. If the child learns the material, proceed to the next step.

If the child does not learn it, there's no harm done. You can just continue for a while, saying and doing the things that prepare the child for the 3 Rs, or for any one or two of the 3 Rs, because the teachable moment can be subject specific. For example, a young child may start reading in November, catch on to counting in February, but show no inclination toward writing until April.

Some early readers show little interest in early arithmetic. Some children who are verbally and quantitatively gifted have difficulties with the fine motor skills needed for writing. Some children who like to draw and scribble will walk away from sorting activities. Progress in all 3 Rs does not necessarily come all at once. So you may find yourself going forward with phonics for one child, with printing for another, and with counting for still another.

Also, children's learning is highly dependent upon method. Some primary pupils do not learn well from the methods of basal textbooks, but they do learn well from individualized early childhood methods that are developmentally appropriate.

Many young children have taken the first steps into reading, writing, and arithmetic with personalized one-on-one teaching for a few minutes a day. In the next unit, I describe how to use the easiest personalized methods to help your pupils take their first steps into the 3 Rs.

9

◆ ◆ ◆

Summary of Unit I

HOW TO FOSTER GROWTH TOWARD READING, WRITING, AND ARITHMETIC

Because language is the basis of all learning, the language of the 3 Rs has to be the starting point for preparing young children for reading, writing, and arithmetic. Since you aim to prepare your pupils for an early start on the 3 Rs, you want to use all of the following strategies every day.

Immerse Them in the Oral Language of the 3 Rs

The oral vocabulary that some young children acquire may contain many basic words connected with food, clothing, and shelter, but very few words connected with reading, writing, and arithmetic. When you immerse these children in the oral language of the 3 Rs, however, they will gain facility in responding to and using the words they need.

Speak Arithme-Talk to Develop Concepts

The language of the 3 Rs includes arithme-talk. By blending your arithme-talk into routine class activities, you will help your girls and boys build concepts connected with sizes, shapes, quantities, measurements, and counting.

Read Aloud to Them, With Participation Extras

When you read aloud and promote conversations about books and the illustrations in them, your children will respond by listening, remembering, and talking about stories, letters, and numbers. When you add extras at read-aloud time, you can get your children to participate in the reading.

Get Them Ready for Phonics—Orally

In preparation for associating sounds with letters, your pupils need to develop phonemic awareness. They need to be able to hear individual sounds in words. When you play sound games with them orally, you enable them to progress toward phonics.

Surround Them With Written Language, and Talk About Print

For print to be meaningful, children have to grasp the connection between the spoken words they hear and the written words they see. In a room filled with many kinds of print, especially environmental print, you can show the connection, and you can arrange activities where the children interact with the print.

Demonstrate Writing, and Talk About Whatever They Write

Whenever you write, talk about what you are doing. Explain your purpose. Read aloud everything you write. If you provide a wide variety of writing materials, and if you build on the starting point of the children's efforts, your pupils will progress toward writing.

Seize the Teachable Moment

Because each child's progress is subject-specific and dependent on instructional method, you must be observant to pick up indicators of teachable moments. As soon as you spot any promising sign, you want to try leading that child into early reading, writing, or arithmetic.

Unit II

♦ ♦ ♦

How to Help Early Learners Take Their First Steps Into the 3 Rs

10

◆ ◆ ◆

Preview of Unit II: Help
With the First Steps

Progress is happening! Your preparatory steps are paying off. Some of your
children are showing you that they can move from random learning in your
print-rich room to focused learning of a few specific words and numbers.

Maybe one of your pupils has almost memorized "The Three Billy Goats
Gruff," and is asking about specific words in the story. Maybe another is trying to write a counting book about billy goats. For these children, and for
others like them, it's time to take the first steps into the 3 Rs. Your goal is to
offer each preschooler the best possible chance to learn by the easiest possible methods.

WHAT TO DO

You should give each child a minute or two a day (or every other day) of personalized, individualized teaching. When your other pupils are busy at centers
for independent activities, you can spend a little structured, personalized time
with each pupil who can benefit from early instruction in reading, writing, or
arithmetic.

And what happens during your private minutes with an early learner?
What do you teach, as a child progresses from preparatory activities to the
early first steps in the 3Rs?

Let's preview the answers to those questions, as they are given in the following chapters. Let's look at what you would do with a pupil named Sonya.

Chapter 11: You would teach Sonya to read these four personally meaningful words, that you will use again in storybook writing with Sonya and in your introduction of phonics:

- Sonya (her own first name)
- Mommy
- called
- Your name (Let's say Ms. Lee.)

Chapter 12: With these four words, you and Sonya will make sentences for her personalized storybook, that she will help to write:

- Mommy called Ms. Lee.
- Ms. Lee called Sonya.
- Sonya called Mommy.

With the addition of one more word, the word for Sonya's favorite food (apples), which is what all the phone calling is about, you will have the makings of Sonya's first personalized storybook.

Chapter 13: Now it's phonics time for Sonya. You will get her started on connecting these sounds with initial letters of familiar words:

- The sound sssss (written /s/) at the beginning of Sonya
- The sound /m/ at the beginning of Mommy
- The sound /k/ at the beginning of called

Chapter 14: You will read aloud and discuss many counting books with Sonya before you help her model on them and construct a personalized "1, 2, 3" book, that will show the numbers in terms of her favorite food, apples.

Chapter 15: Sonya will select additional words she wants to learn to read. Many of these words are likely to be proper nouns (the names of people she likes) and action verbs. You will help Sonya write more words and more numbers in personalized books about herself.

Chapter 16: Sonya will learn more sound-letter relationships that are connected with the initial letters of her self-selected words, as she progresses in phonics.

With each child who can benefit from early instruction in reading, writing, or arithmetic, you can take the steps that are described in the "Sonya" example here. These are the steps that enable a young learner to get an early start on the 3 Rs:

- Teach each beginning reader four words.
- Help the child write a personalized story.

- Connect familiar initial letters with their sounds.
- Make a personalized "1, 2, 3" book with each early learner.
- Introduce more child-selected numbers, words, and personalized books.
- Use child-selected words for teaching more phonics.

The learnings in chapter 11 must precede those in chapters 12 and 13. Your child has to recognize four words before he or she can use the words to write a personalized story, or connect the initial letters of the four words with their sounds.

Some children, however, may come to identify and comprehend the numbers 1, 2, and 3 before they recognize any words. For those children, the counting book activity in chapter 14 might precede the literacy activities in chapters 11, 12, and 13.

Chapters 15 and 16 build on previous chapters' discussions.

WHY TO DO IT

The first words a child speaks are names of meaningful persons and objects. It follows linguistically that the first words spoken should also be the first words read. The rationale is clear for choosing the child's own name and the word *Mommy* as two of the first four words for the preschooler to learn to read. Your own name (as the child's teacher) also fits in the names category.

Reading sentences, rather than individual words, is a step that beginners need to take as soon as possible. Children should move quickly from regarding reading as identifying a string of words, one by one, to regarding reading as gaining meaning from sentences.

The individualized and personalized teaching approach is best for young children because they are egocentric. Each one often wants and expects your undivided attention, because each one is operating only from his or her own limited perspective. At this stage, the one-on-one teacher–pupil situation gives each child the best opportunity to learn. Most of the early first steps are designed for individualized, personalized teaching. This focused but undemanding approach enables you to help your pupils make easy transitions from informal, unstructured, preparatory activities to early first-step activities in each of the 3 Rs.

Consider the first R, reading. At the preparatory stage, you introduced signs and labels (environmental print), in hopes that the child would learn to recognize a few favorites.

At the first-steps stage, you will teach four specific words (two that are the child's name and your name), in hopes that the child will learn to read those words in sentences.

Consider writing. At the preparatory stage, you showed each pupil the many uses of writing, and happily accepted scribbles, in hopes that the child would see the functions of written communication.

At the first-steps stage, you will enable your pupil to become the author of a personalized storybook, in hopes that the child will do some of the printing, and will want to continue "authoring."

Consider arithmetic. At the preparatory stage, you spoke arithme-talk, in hopes that the child would develop concepts of quantity that would lead to counting.

At the first-steps stage, you will help your pupil associate the concepts of one, two, and three with the symbols 1, 2, and 3 in a personalized counting book, in hopes that the child will learn to connect the printed numbers with the quantities.

The early first steps into the 3 Rs help a child move from random learning to focused learning. Preparatory activities brought about random learning. They were like scattershot, aiming at a wide range of possibilities. They supported the learning of whatever words the child spontaneously recognized, letters the child tried to print, or arithmetic concepts registered to the child.

Your first-step activities will support the learning of four specific words to read and write, four specific letter-sound relationships in phonics, and three specific numbers to count. Obviously, these specifics are nowhere near as heavy or demanding as the specifics of primary basal programs, but they are definitely not random. They are well defined and focused.

If a young child learns these few specifics, that child is at a growth point on the emergent literacy continuum. Very few preschoolers learn to recognize four words on wordcards, and then stop. They usually want more words. They often show interest in learning to read the names of all their family members, friends, pets, and favorite foods, plus the verbs for their favorite activities (swim, hop, somersault).

Similarly, the early learner who makes the breakthrough of mastering the "one, two, three" counting concepts can progress soon to "four" and "five" and higher numbers. The children who stack, nest, match, sort, measure, and weigh at early ages may begin to talk about what they are doing, and apply their learnings to arithmetic.

The early writer often progresses simultaneously in letter formation and letter-sound relationships, especially when each new letter is the initial letter of a word of special interest to the child. Self-selection of the early reading and writing vocabulary is essential in early instruction in the 3 Rs. Young children easily learn what they are eager to learn when the material is presented in a developmentally appropriate manner.

The early first steps are not just traditional first-grade methods moved down into kindergarten or nursery school. They are designed especially for younger children who show signs that they can benefit from instruction in reading, writing, or arithmetic at early ages. Because the early first steps require only a minimum amount of prior learning, they also work well with immature primary grade pupils who have not succeeded in traditional basal programs.

The experts who view emergent literacy as a continuum emphasize that each child travels along this continuum at his or her own individual pace. Usually you can expect a 5-year-old to travel faster than a 3-year-old. But some 3-year-olds will surprise you. A 3-year-old from a rich literacy background may make faster progress than a 5-year-old from a deprived literacy background.

Even the most precocious beginners will have standstills as well as spurts of progress in early reading or writing or arithmetic. The chapters in this unit will show you how to personalize your teaching so as to "hold each child's hand" for the early first steps into the 3 Rs.

11

◆ ◆ ◆

Teach Each Beginning
Reader Four Words

Overview

These are the topics you will meet in this chapter:

- Timing and Materials
- Recognizing the First Word, the Child's Name
- Distinguishing the Word *Mommy* From the Child's Name
- Preparing for and Presenting the Third Word
- Teaching Recognition of the Teacher's Name
- Moving from Wordcards to Sentences

TIMING AND MATERIALS

The best way to find out for sure if a child can benefit from early reading instruction is to try to teach the child to read these four words:

- the child's first name
- Mommy
- called
- your name

If the child learns the words, then that child is capable of taking the early first steps into reading. If the child does not learn the words, then you should have that child continue with the preparatory activities described in Unit I until he or she is further along the emergent-literacy continuum.

To give a child a good chance at learning each word, try to spend about a minute a day, teaching the child individually. If within a couple of weeks to a month (depending on the age of the child), your pupil does not learn to recognize and distinguish among the four words, discontinue your efforts and try again later. Maybe the child needs more exposure to environmental print. Maybe read-aloud times will trigger the child's desire to learn to read later in the year. Proceed only with those children who show both the ability and the inclination to learn to read at early ages.

Wordcards (or flashcards) are the easiest materials you can use to teach a child the first four words. Even if the child's name and your name are not phonetically regular, they can be learned by sight from wordcards. Start with wordcards first and proceed thereafter to phonics.

When you make a wordcard for the word *Mommy*, print it on an index card. Remember to capitalize the first letter of *Mommy* and to use lower-case letters for the rest of the word, because that is the way the word usually appears in print. Also, you will capitalize only the first letter for the child's first name and your name. The word *called* should be printed in all lower-case letters, because it will be used in the middles of sentences between proper nouns.

RECOGNIZING THE FIRST WORD, THE CHILD'S NAME

During your preparatory activities, you encouraged all your children to try to print their names, so you have established some background for name recognition. But real *reading recognition* may not have occurred yet. It is not uncommon for a very young child to surmise that everything in print is his or her name.

It is quite common for children to use the capital letters at the beginnings of their names as the defining clue for word recognition. For example, a young child named Lazaro might call every word that starts with a capital L "Lazaro," or a Naomi might call every word that starts with N "Naomi." Such children are moving in the direction of reading, but need your individualized teaching to be able to discriminate between words.

You want all of them to reach reading recognition of their names. So, you should start your first individualized lesson by giving your pupil a hand mirror with his or her name taped on it. Say to the child:

> *You see yourself in the mirror.*
> *You see your name on the card.*
> *You can read your name from the card.*
> *Let's hear you read it.* (Child reads name.)
> *Yes, the word on the card is your name.*
> *That's a word you can read.*

Soon your pupils will no longer need the mirror for a clue. Then review the name frequently from the card alone.

If you label the child's belongings, use the same form of the name (capitalized first letter and lower-case printing for the rest of the letters). Have the child practice name-reading from boots, jackets, sweaters, and all other labeled items, as well as from the wordcard.

Show the child every place in the room where you have printed his or her name—on the attendance chart, the helpers list, the chalkboard. Have the child go to those places and point to his or her name, and copy it.

To reinforce reading by writing, the child might trace the letters in the name, or copy the name in chalk, crayon, paint, pencil, and felt-tip pen. Don't be concerned if some of your children print their names in all capital letters. That's a start. Capitals seem easier than lower-case letters for early writers. But you want the name on your wordcard to look like the name in print, so during your minutes of one-on-one reading instruction, stay with a capital for the first letter and lower-case for the other letters. That way, the transfer from reading the name on a wordcard to reading the name on labels to reading it in print will be easier.

Some names are phonetically regular, such as Ed, Bo, and Nan. Others are not, such as Phil, Mignon, and Sean (pronounced Shawn). At this first-step stage, use whatever background your pupil has in the letter-sound relationships of phonics only if the association of letters and sounds will aid the child in recognizing his or her name.

When your pupil's recognition seems fairly firm, move on to the second word, Mommy, and continue to review the child's name.

DISTINGUISHING THE WORD MOMMY FROM THE CHILD'S NAME

Point out that in person Mommy and the child look different, and that in print the words Mommy and the child's name look different, too. You could present the word Mommy on its wordcard after discussing with your early reader what Mommy does in the morning (breakfast, dressing, driving). Say to the child:

> *This is the word Mommy.*
> *Let's read it together—Mommy.*
> *Take a good look at it. Now you hold*
> *the card. Tell me what word is on it.*
> *Yes, it's the word Mommy. You're reading!*
> *Now I'm going to point to the word and*
> *I want you to read it to me again.*

Reward your child with praise whenever he or she looks at the card and says *Mommy.* Mommy is a relatively easy word for a beginner to learn because the child can associate it with someone extremely important. Because all of your early readers are learning the word *Mommy,* you will be reviewing it frequently.

If you are the child's mother, as well as teacher, it will be easy for you to review the Mommy card frequently. You might wear it pinned to your skirt. You might prop it up by your plate at mealtime. All you have to do is point to the card and say, "I'm Mommy, and this is the word *Mommy,*" and you have created a lesson.

You may notice that some children confuse *Mommy* and their own names and have trouble telling the two wordcards apart. Most of the time, this is just an extension of the child's erroneous idea that everything in print is his or her name. More interaction with environmental print will help dispel that notion.

The confusion, however, would be very understandable for a girl named Mary or a boy named Manny because those names start with capital M and are similar in configuration to the word *Mommy.* For any child whose name begins with M, there may be confusion. It is a good idea, therefore, to substitute *Daddy* or *Grandma* as the second word for those children.

Whatever way you decide to handle that difficulty, if it should arise, remember that distinguishing between two words in print is a giant step for a beginner. The necessary degree of visual discrimination won't fall into place overnight for all your pupils. Some children learn *Mommy* at a glance and request another word immediately. But others may need many repeated one-minute daily sessions to remember the word on the card, or to tell the difference between their own names and the word *Mommy.*

One toddler surprised both his mother and his nursery-school teacher in the way he showed that he could read the word *Mommy* from a wordcard. The teacher had been talking with him about the word on its card every day during their one-minute individualized times together.

At the classroom door one morning, as the toddler's mother was leaving him off, she said to her little son, "Kiss Mommy good-by."

The child picked up the *Mommy* card from his teacher's desk and kissed it. Real reading recognition had occurred for the word *Mommy,* no doubt about it!

When your teaching seems to take, and your child is comfortably distinguishing between the *Mommy* wordcard and the wordcard for his or her name, then move on to the third word, *called.* But continue to review the reading of the word *Mommy* and the child's name every day.

PREPARING FOR AND PRESENTING
THE THIRD WORD

Build background for the word *called* by collecting as many toy telephones as possible for use in your classroom. Then you are ready to talk about phone calls and to play games that involve calling on the phone. (At other times you will probably use the phones to work with numbers and letters, but at this point you are using them strictly to prepare for the presentation of the word *called*, the all-important third word that will enable your pupils to make sentences from their wordcards.) Have the children use the telephones to pretend to call home, to call friends, to call you.

Play the guessing game, "Who called?" Your pupils may think this is just a game of identifying voices on the phone, but it is really a part of the preparation for learning to recognize the word *called*. It promotes the oral use of the word, so the children will have heard and spoken the word *called* before they learn to read it.

In this game the teacher turns away from a small group of students so that she cannot see which one is calling her on a toy phone. (Let's name the teacher Ms. Lee.) One student presses the buttons to place a phone call to the teacher and then asks the teacher, "Who called Ms. Lee?"

Ms. Lee listens carefully to the voice of the questioner and tries to identify the student by voice. She says, "Alison called Ms. Lee," or "Juanita called Ms. Lee," as she comes up with the correct identification (let's hope).

In this game, the teacher speaks the very sentences that Alison and Juanita will soon read—when they learn to recognize the word *called*.

For even stronger preparation, try to reverse roles with your pupils in the "Who Called?" game. Have one of them do the identifying by voice. Be sure, of course, that you are in the game, to be identified as a caller. Suppose Alison, for example, recognized her teacher's voice in the game and said, "Ms. Lee called Alison." She has spoken a sentence that she will soon be on her way toward reading.

After this oral preparation, you are ready to present the word *called* on a wordcard. Even though you have played the "Who Called?" game with small groups of children, you will want to introduce the word on its wordcard in a one-on-one situation.

During your individual minute with a child you are teaching, you might hold up the *called* wordcard and say:

> This is the word <u>called</u>. Earlier today
> we played the game, "Who called?"
> So you've heard the word <u>called</u> before.
> You've spoken it too. I knew your voice
> when you asked, "Who called Ms. Lee?"
> Now you're going to read the word <u>called</u>.
> on this wordcard. Let's read it together.
> Now you read it by yourself.

Point out the configuration of the word *called*, as contrasted with *Mommy*. Their shapes are quite different. Keep the introduction short, but review the word frequently.

Many children take a longer time to master *called* than *Mommy* or their own names. That's understandable, since a verb in the past tense is less concrete than proper nouns. Also, *called* lacks the emotional connections of *Mommy* and the child's own name. But most early learners will come to recognize their third word, just as they did the first two.

When your child can distinguish among the three words that you have taught (the child's name, the word *Mommy*, and the word *called*), it's time to demonstrate how you can put the wordcards in two different orders to make these two different sentences:

Mommy	called	child's name

Child's name	called	Mommy

At first, the child may read these two sentences with no intonation. They'll sound just like a list of unrelated words. But after you teach one more word (your name), you will take time to model the reading of sentences that have the word *called* in the middle. Then your pupil's reading intonation will begin to sound more natural, more like the intonation of speech.

TEACHING RECOGNITION
OF THE TEACHER'S NAME

On the wordcard for your name, print whatever you have your pupils call you. If you have posted that same name on the door of your print-rich room, you can start the individualized lesson on your name by pointing out the posting. Your pupil may already have noticed your name in print on the door and may have built some visual familiarity with it.

Perhaps you have also been wearing your name on a sticky label. If so, point out to your pupil that your name looks the same in print on the door, on the sticky label, and now on the wordcard that you present to the child.

Have the child add your name to his or her collection of *Mommy*, *called*, and the child's first name. Now your pupil has four word cards.

To reinforce the reading of your name, you might ask your child to find it in all the places where it appears. If you have labeled all your belongings with your name, just as the children's belongings are labeled with their names, your pupil should come up with quite a few appearances of your name.

Many teachers go by Ms., Miss, Mrs., or Mr. in front of the last name. So it is likely that your child has two wordcards on which capital M is the initial letter. This gives the child an opportunity (and a need) to develop visual discrimination between your name and *Mommy*.

To help your pupil, you want to point out as many differences as possible between your name and the word *Mommy*. You will definitely want to talk about

the length and configuration of the words on the two wordcards, the capital letter at the beginning of your proper name, and the space between the title Ms. or
Mr. and your name. These differences will help your pupil discriminate between
the word *Mommy* and your name.

In case you are the child's mother as well as teacher, you might teach the
name of a neighbor who is addressed as Ms. or Mr., so that your child will still
have four wordcards.

MOVING FROM WORDCARDS TO SENTENCES

When your early reader can discriminate among the four words you have
taught, it is time for the child to have some sentence-reading practice. Your pupil will enjoy reading all the different sentences that can be made with just a
name at the beginning, a name at the end, and the word *called* in the middle.

To continue with our examples of Ms. Lee and Alison, you can generate
these sentences:

> Alison called Ms. Lee.
> Alison called Mommy.
> Mommy called Alison.
> Mommy called Ms. Lee.
> Ms. Lee called Mommy.
> Ms. Lee called Alison.

If your pupil makes long pauses between words when reading the sentences
made from wordcards, you will need to reread the sentence for the child. You
can demonstrate intonation when grouping words into sentences, so oral reading sounds like natural speaking. Encourage the child to copy your intonation.
You want every early learner to read with expression and to group words meaningfully.

Now you are ready to help your pupil become the author of a personalized
storybook, a book where all the words are familiar and easy to recognize, a book
that the child is certain to be able to read, and can help to write.

Congratulations on the great teaching job you are doing!

12

◆　◆　◆

Help Each Child Write
a Personalized Storybook

Overview

These are the topics you will meet in this chapter:

• Personalized, Short, and Easy to Read
• Preparation for Authoring
• Making the Pages
• Ongoing Benefits of Personalized Books

PERSONALIZED, SHORT, AND EASY TO READ

If a child can print his or her first name, the child is ready for early writing instruction by this *personalized storybook* method. The story is told in the four words your pupil can already read—the words *Mommy, called,* your name, and the child's first name. These words appear in the three sentences that tell the story. The child will definitely be able to read the personalized storybook that he or she writes, because all the words will have been learned in advance.

Each pupil can print as much or as little of the story as you see fit. You know the individual abilities of your pupils. Your least skilled writer might print only his or her name in the book to personalize the story. A more advanced pupil might print all three sentences. It's up to you.

Each personalized storybook will be three to five pages long. The pages should be stapled together along the left side, just as a book is bound. Whatever size paper you use, bind the pages horizontally (as in landscape on a computer) rather than vertically (as in portrait on a computer). The extra width allows for more writing space.

The first page is the cover.

The second page (or the second, third, and fourth pages) will contain the three sentences that tell the story. Some early learners do better with only one sentence per page, so their teachers lengthen the book accordingly.

The last page is the grand finale, and features the child's favorite food.

PREPARATION FOR AUTHORING

Before you present your pupil with the exciting prospect of authoring a personalized storybook, you need to prepare the child. As is true of many low-vocabulary stories, the plot is skeletal, so you and your early learner will need to converse about the story in advance. You will supply much of the plot so you can lead the child into this reading and writing experience with ease and comfort.

One approach to preparation is to play a pretend game with the child. You can set up a corner of your room for pretending by putting three toy telephones on three chairs in a triangle. Then sit in the first chair and hold the telephone. Have your pupil do the same with the second chair. Put a doll, representing the child's mother, in the third chair with a phone. Say:

> *Let's pretend it's the weekend.*
> *You are at home by your phone.*
> *I am in my home with my phone.*
> *Your mommy went to the grocery store.*
> *After she shopped, she called me*
> *on the phone from a friend's house.*

When you and the child are situated in your chairs, you can put the Mommy wordcard beside the doll, to establish identity. Then, continue to describe the pretend situation by saying:

> *Let's pretend our way through three*
> *phone calls. First, let's pretend that*
> *when your mommy called me, she told me*
> *she bought something at the grocery store*
> *that you really like.*
> *Next, I called you on the phone and told you*
> *your mommy had bought a treat for you,*
> *but I didn't know what it was.*

*Then you called your mommy to find out
what it was.
What would you want the treat to be?*

This pretending leads up to the actual writing (printing) of three sentences for the personalized storybook. As mentioned earlier in this unit, if your name were Ms. Lee and the child's name was Sonya, the sentences would be:

*Mommy called Ms. Lee.
Ms. Lee called Sonya.
Sonya called Mommy.*

The last page of the book features the label, name, or picture of the child's favorite treat, so the book is truly personalized.

You may want a child to play this pretend game repeatedly, at first just with you, but later with another child, rather than a doll, taking the role of the mother. Or perhaps you feel that it would be better in your class to dramatize the pretend situation for a group of children. Whatever way you handle it, be sure to set the scene before you start on the actual construction of the book.

MAKING THE PAGES

With some of your early writers, you will need to lengthen your one minute individualized lessons on the days you make the first personalized book. Only you know how much help each child needs. So only you can decide what words you should print, which ones the child should print, and how many sessions the authoring project should occupy.

As you start on the first page (the cover page), you want to present the project as a joint effort. So you print the book title "Mommy" on the cover, and your pupil prints his or her name as the author. To encourage the child to do this printing, you might say:

*This is the cover of the book we are
going to make together. The title is
"Mommy" since it's about your mommy
getting something for you. You can
print your name here as author.*

The next page (or pages) show the sentences about the three phone calls, so you should review them from the pretend game. Provide time for the child to ask questions and make comments.

Have the child's wordcards nearby so you and your pupil can set up the sentences about the telephoning. You'll need three copies of the *called* wordcard and two copies of each of the other cards if you want to show all three sentences.

With some of your children, you may want to use three separate pages for the three sentences, since their printing may go all over the page. With others, who may be older, neater, or more legible, one page will provide enough room for all three sentences. One page is also adequate if the child wants you to do most of the printing.

If you draw lines across the top, middle, and bottom of one page for the sentences, use the lines as guides only for your printing, and not for your pupil's printing. Beginners have trouble staying on the lines.

Your most capable pupils may want to print all three sentences, after you set up the wordcards for copying. But other children will print only a word or two, and you'll print the rest.

> Mommy called (teacher's name).
> (Teacher's name) called (child's name).
> (Child's name) called Mommy.

After you review the events behind the first sentence, in which the mother called you on the phone, set up the three wordcards. Then ask your child, "Do you want to print all the words? Or just the first word, *Mommy?*"

Whatever way the printing gets done, be sure to have your pupil read the completed sentence aloud to you, for example, "Mommy called Ms. Lee." You might then ask, for example, "And who did Ms. Lee call?" Most pupils will remember that their teacher called them.

After this oral discussion leads up to the second sentence, you can print your name at the beginning to reinforce who is doing the calling. It might then read, for example, "Ms. Lee called _____ (child's name)." Try to have the pupil print at least his or her name at the end of that sentence. Then have the child read both the first and the second sentences back to you.

Use the same procedures for the third sentence. That's the sentence in which the child called Mommy to find out what treat she bought at the grocery store.

After the child reads back all three sentences, you supply the name, label, picture, or drawing of the treat for the last page of the storybook.

The personalized books that your children make from these pages may vary greatly, of course, according to their printing capabilities and food choices for the final pages.

ONGOING BENEFITS OF PERSONALIZED BOOKS

Each pupil's personalized book represents a successful authoring experience that you created for the child. That is the most important element of this project. You're willing to go to great lengths to help each of your early learners be-come an author because you know that the child's first personalized book will be the first of many.

Personalized books are a very important part of early 3 Rs programs. They serve well as first-step instructional materials not only in early reading and writ-ing but also in arithmetic, as you will soon see, through the personalized count-ing book.

They can also serve to keep parents informed of their children's progress, so you want each early learner to take home the personalized storybook and read it aloud. Something very gratifying may happen at home. The child may be re-warded with the treat featured on the last page of the book.

13

♦ ♦ ♦

Connect Familiar Initial
Letters With Their Sounds

Overview

These are the topics you will meet in this chapter:

- From the First Four Words to Phonics
- Phonics Practice on Paper
- Other Words in Print That Start With Familiar Sounds
- Preparation for Blending Sounds Into Words
- Using Early Phonics for Interactive Writing

FROM THE FIRST FOUR WORDS
TO PHONICS

Many phonics programs set out right from the start to teach the sounds of all the letters of the alphabet. For your early learners, the aim of the first steps into phonics is much more modest. If a pupil learns just three or four letter-sound relationships through your personalized approach, that child is off to a good start on the first steps.

Each of your early readers can already recognize four words by sight: *Mommy, called*, the child's own name, and your name. It makes sense, therefore, to start into phonics by teaching the letter-sound relationship of the letter M and the sound mmmmm (written /m/) as in *Mommy*. You can also teach the connection between the letter c and its sound (written /k/), as in the sight word *called*, and the sounds of the initial letters of the child's and your name.

When you spot a teachable moment for leading a child into phonics, take out the *Mommy* wordcard again. Point to the capital M at the beginning of the word and say:

The letter M stands for the sound /m/. The word
Mommy starts with the sound /m/ and the letter M.

Have the child repeat the sound /m/ after you—mmmmmmmm. Say "Mmmmmommy," stretching out the initial sound to emphasize it. Have the child trace the letter M with his or her finger when making the sound /m/.

After the child grasps the connection between the sound /m/ and the letter M, you can use the same procedure to teach the sound /k/ as in *called*, the sound of the first letter of the child's name (for example, /s/ as in Sonya), and the sound of your initial (for example, /l/ as in Ms. Lee).

Phonics Practice on Paper

Some of your pupils will benefit from phonics practice with four letters on paper. To personalize this practice for each pupil, you can fold a piece of paper in half and then in half again to make four sections. In the first section, print the letter for the child's initial. In the second section, print the capital letter M, as in *Mommy*. In the third section, print c, as in *called*. In the last section, print the letter for your initial, assuming that you and your pupil have worked on that letter and its sound.

Then you can point at the first letter of the child's name and ask for the sound of that letter. In fact, you can ask quite a few questions about the letter-sound relationships of the initial letters of the early reader's first four words. As you and your child look at the four sections of the paper with a letter in each section, you might ask:

- *Which letter does the word Mommy start with?*
- *Which letter stands for the sound /k/?*
- *The name of this letter is M. What is its sound?*
- *Point to the letter that your name starts with.*
- *What is the sound of that letter? What is its name?*

Other Words in Print That Start With Familiar Sounds

As a precursor to phonics, you built your pupils' phonemic awareness of sounds in words. You used the oral approach, so that each pupil would hear and say sounds before trying to connect sounds with letters in print. Now, to help a child take the first steps into phonics, you are adding print. Oral phonemic awareness is good preparation for phonics, but connecting letters in print with their sounds is phonics in action.

Suppose a pupil can *hear* that the name *Matt* starts with the same sound as *Mommy*. That pupil now needs to *see* that *Mommy* and *Matt* start with the same letter, M. To help the child grasp the letter-sound relationship, you might write *Matt* alongside *Mommy* on the board and say,

> *The names <u>Matt</u> and <u>Mommy</u> start with the same sound /m/. They also start with the same letter, M. See the M at the beginning of <u>Mommy</u> and <u>Matt</u>.*

Ask your pupils for additional words that start with the sound /m/. If they come up with *monkey, Mexico, Melissa,* and *money,* write each word on the board, pointing out the letter M or m at the beginning of each word. Your pupils do not need to read back all the words. They just need to register on the initial letter M/m that says "mmmmm."

At this point you need to explain that the capital and lower-case forms of a letter (e.g., the "big M" and the "little m") stand for the same sound. A child who has watched Sesame Street regularly may recognize the "M/m" connection because of the repeated presentations on the program.

Look at your collection of environmental print. Do you have any signs, labels, menus, or containers that show words which start with the letter M? If so, pull them out. Show them to your early learner. Point out the initial letter M and the sound /m/ on each word.

Play guessing games. "I spy something that starts with the letter M." On each guess that a student offers, elongate the sound of the initial /m/ as you repeat the word. "Mmmmop. Mmmmilk. Mmmmman."

Use these same strategies as you work on the letter-sound connections of the child's and your initials.

Some letters, of course, can stand for more than one sound. If you have both a *George* and a *Gail* among your pupils, you will see the benefit of individualizing your instruction for the first steps into phonics. George will take his first steps into phonics by learning that his initial G stands for the sound /j/. Gail will take her first steps by learning that her initial G stands for the sound /g/.

Later on, of course, both George and Gail will learn more about phonics, including the fact that the letter G can stand for both a hard sound (/g/ as in Gail) and a soft sound (/j/ as in George). These first steps in phonics are just a start, but a highly personalized start. George and Gail benefit by having their names as reference points for one of their earliest letter-sound associations.

Connecting the letter c (as in *called*) with the sound /k/ is a harder job than showing pupils the connection between the letter M and the sound /m/. You can list many common words that start with c (*cat, cake, candy, cot, color, cook, cube*), and point out the letter-sound connection of c and /k/.

But when you ask your pupils for other words that start with the sound /k/, they may come up with *kitten* and *kite*. Accept such words, but list them separately from the words that start with c. You can explain that both c and k stand for the sound /k/. Then tell your child, "But today we're looking just at the letter c and its sound."

PREPARATION FOR BLENDING
SOUNDS INTO WORDS

After you have started a child on the first steps into phonics, you want to continue to develop the child's phonemic awareness, especially in the area of blending. Phonics is useful for reading only if the child can blend sounds into words. Therefore, you may want to make repeated use of a guessing game where your pupils will combine context clues and phonemic awareness.

To play this game, you need to establish a category of words as your context clues. Using farm animals, for example, as your category for context, you might tell your pupil:

I'm going to say all the sounds in the name
of a farm animal—/p/ /i/ /g/. What animal is it?

You will, of course, separate the /p/ from the /i/ from the /g/ so that you are making three distinct sounds. If your pupil does not understand, you will need to say the sounds again, closer together. If the child still looks confused or blank, keep repeating the sounds, closer and closer together, until you blend them into the word *pig*, to demonstrate what you are teaching.

The child who can immediately answer "pig" is showing strong phonemic awareness. Most beginners need repeated oral demonstrations from you to catch on to the idea of blending sounds into words. It is a big step also to move from hearing and understanding to doing. Many young children take a long time to apply blending to reading.

To continue the game with more farm animals, you might tell your child:

I'm going to say all the sounds in
the name of another farm animal—
/g/ /ō/ /t/. What animal is it? (goat)
/sh/ /ē/ /p/. What animal is it? (sheep)
/l/ /a/ /m/. What is it? (lamb)

Note that the game addresses sounds only, not the letters for spelling a word. It is strictly an oral game. It involves no print, no naming of letters. There are four letters in the word *goat* but only three sounds, and five letters in *sheep*, but only three sounds.

The child who catches on immediately may want to be leader in the next round of the game. That pupil might ask the other children, "What farm animal is this—/h/ /e/ /n/?" (hen)

You may want to change the category (context clue) to "creatures that can fly," and ask:

What creature is this—/b/ /ē/?   (bee)
What creature is this—/d/ /u/ /k/?   (duck)
What creature is this—/d/ /u/ /v/?   (dove)

The game works best with short one-syllable words. Consonant blends should be separated because they are two distinct sounds. For the word *snail*, for example, you would say /s/ /n/ /ā/ /l/. Consonant digraphs, of course, cannot be separated because they are one sound; for the word *chick*, you would say /ch/ /i/ /k/.

This blending game mimics what beginning readers must do when they try to decode an unfamiliar word by "sounding it out" with phonics. If they become accustomed to the blending concept orally, it will be easier for them to blend sounds into words in print.

USING EARLY PHONICS
FOR INTERACTIVE WRITING

The first steps into phonics focus primarily on the initial letters of the four sight words your early reader knows from wordcards. Each early reader learns the letter-sound relationship of the letter M and the sound /m/, of the letter c and the sound /k/, and of the initial letters of the child's and your names.

In these steps, you also help the child apply these four letter-sound relationships to other words that start with or contain the familiar letters. Suppose, for example, that a child wanted to write the name *Mickey* and asked you how to spell it. Instead of just dictating the letters to the child or immediately writing *Mickey* on a wordcard and handing it over, you could help the child apply the first steps into phonics by using this interactive writing approach.

You could say, "Let's say that name slowly, Mmmmickey. What sound do you hear at the beginning?"

The child should reply, "Mmmmmmm."

"What letter stands for that sound?"

The child should reply, "M."

"Because Mickey is a name, we want to use a capital M at the beginning. Where do you see a capital M in our room?"

Some children will still need help with finding the letter M in your print-rich room. But others can probably locate it quickly and copy it, or form it from memory.

Possibly you might get additional phonics mileage from the name *Mickey*, if you asked about the sound /k/ in the middle of the name. Your early learner has started connecting the letter c (as in *called*) with the sound /k/, but only in the initial position. In the name Mickey, you have the sound /k/ in the middle of the word.

Perhaps you'd like to find out if your early learner can deal with a medial sound. Remember that some children cannot yet focus on a sound in the middle of a word; they are still struggling with initial sounds. But if you have a pupil who is advancing rapidly in phonics and in writing, you might try this approach:

> *There is another sound you know in the middle of the name Mickey. You figured out that Mickey starts with the sound /m/ and the letter M. You printed the big M very well.*
> *I wonder if you can figure out what letter is in the middle of Mickey. Listen—Mickey.*

(Emphasize the sound /k/ as you say the name.)

> *Isn't that the sound that the word called starts with?*
> *What is the letter for that sound?*

Whether the child answers with the letter c or the letter k, the answer is correct for the name Mickey, because both letters are in the middle. You can point out either or both letters as you help your pupil print the rest of the name Mickey.

This approach will work with some children and not with others. But it's worth an occasional try to see how far each pupil can go into interactive writing with the first steps in phonics. Even for the pupils who are very quick to catch on to letter-sound relationships, there is still value in continuing the phonemic awareness games that promote blending. The oral blending games get them ready to use phonics effectively in writing and reading.

You will teach additional letter-sound relationships as the child learns to recognize more words. As always, the teaching needs to be individualized and personalized because each child will ask for different words.

Just as it is easiest for early learners to recognize the self-selected nouns and verbs that are most familiar and interesting to them, it is also easiest in phonics for them to learn the sounds associated with the initial letters of those familiar and personally meaningful words.

14

♦ ♦ ♦

Make a Personalized "1, 2, 3" Book With Each Early Learner

Overview

These are the topics you will meet in this chapter:

- Counting Books
- Concepts Before Symbols
- Arithme-talk at Read-Aloud Time
- Your Demonstration
- All 3 Rs in the Counting Book Project

COUNTING BOOKS

Making a personalized "1, 2, 3" counting book is a project that integrates reading, writing, and arithmetic for early learners.

Your children have probably heard you read many counting books aloud. Because of this background that you have established, your pupils may be ready to model on those counting books, and make their own personalized "1, 2, 3" books. Their individual counting books will include pictures of their favorite foods from the last page of each personalized storybook.

Whatever counting books are available to you can serve as models, because you focus primarily on the first few pages of each book. Some popular titles and authors are:

- Anno, M. *Anno's counting book.* Crowell.
- Berenstain, S. and J. *Bears on wheels.* Random House.
- Bond, M. *Paddington's 1, 2, 3.* Viking.
- Carle, E. *1, 2, 3 to the zoo.* Philomel.
- de Brunhoff, L. *Babar's counting book.* Random House.
- Feelings, M. *Moja means one: Swahili counting book.* Dial.
- Fleming, D. *Count!* Henry Holt.
- Garne, S. T. *One white sail.* Simon & Schuster.
- Kitchen, B. *Animal numbers.* Dial.
- Seymour, B. *First counting.* Walck.
- St. Pierre, S. *The count counts scary things.* Children's Television Workshop Publishing.
- Van Fleet, M. *One yellow lion.* Dial.
- Ziner, F. *Counting carnival.* Putnam & Grossett.

Most counting books feature at least the numbers 1 to 10, and some go higher. Some books also count back down again. Some present groupings of animals and objects in their illustrations, to show the combinations that add up to 5, 6, 7, etc.

As you lead up to your personalized counting book project, however, you want to spend most of your read-aloud time on the pages that feature the numbers 1, 2, and 3. These pages will help your pupils develop their earliest counting concepts, so they are the best preparation for the "1, 2, 3" book.

Concepts Before Symbols

Of course, you want your children's concepts of one, two, and three to be firm before you have them match the concepts with their printed symbols 1, 2, and 3. It's an important step for a child to count aloud, "1, 2, 3," while touching items to show mastery of the one-to-one correspondence.

But it is definitely an additional step, and a more advanced step, for a young child to associate each number concept with its printed symbol. That step brings reading and writing together with arithmetic. Most children can count to three well ahead of the time that they can read, write, and comprehend the symbol 3 in print.

Some children master the concept of one-to-one correspondence in stages. They handle the oral counting of 1, 2, 3 correctly. But they lack the patience or understanding to stay with one-to-one correspondence for the higher numbers, and they orally run them together, saying something like "4, 6, 7, 10." For the early first steps into arithmetic, therefore, you want to limit your requirements to the concepts of one, two, and three. You can use the personalized counting-book project to help your early learners connect the concepts with the printed symbols, 1, 2, and 3.

Arithme-talk at Read-Aloud Time

Suppose, when you are still establishing background at read-aloud time, you are on the "3" page of a counting book about toys. You might say:

> *Look at the kites on this page.*
> *Let's count them aloud together:*
> *1, 2, 3.* (You touch each kite in turn.)
> *Audrey, would you please touch*
> *the kites for me as we count again?*

Only after this oral reviewing of concepts would you point at and identify the printed symbol 3, and say to your pupils:

> *Here in the middle of the page*
> *you can see the number 3.*
> *Let's read it together—3.*
> *Now let's write it together.*
> *Pretend you are finger-painting*
> *a 3 on the back of your hand.*
> *Make two curves.* (Demonstrate.)

After reading and discussing as many counting books as possible, you will want to demonstrate how to personalize the making of a "1, 2, 3" book.

YOUR DEMONSTRATION

The best way you can show your children how to personalize their books is to stand up in front of them and make a counting book yourself. You want to make it clear that your book features your favorite food, since they will use pictures of their favorite foods in their first "1, 2, 3" books. Let's say that your favorite food is oranges.

To prepare for your demonstration, you would need to cut out circles from orange construction paper, so that you would have them ready to paste on three sheets of paper. During your demonstration, you will paste one orange on the first sheet, two oranges on the second, and three on the third. After the pasting, you will label the pages 1, 2, and 3.

To start, you would say to your pupils:

The food I like best is oranges.
So I'm going to make a "1, 2, 3" book
about oranges. Here are the three pages
for my book. I'm going to paste a different
number of oranges on each page.

Pause and do the pasting while the children watch. Then ask the children how many oranges you pasted on each page. After they have correctly answered 1, 2, and 3, you write the proper number on each page in big print.

Then you can put the pages in order and make a cover for your book. Demonstrate the writing of 1, 2, and 3 that you want each pupil to do on the cover. Each child will show authorship of a personalized counting book by printing his or her name in a by-line under the title.

1   2   3
by _____ (child's name)

In your demonstration you print your own name on the cover of your 1, 2, 3 book. Then staple the pages together, and read the finished product to your children. They will be very pleased that you are going to help each of them make a counting book similar to yours.

ALL 3 Rs IN THE COUNTING BOOK PROJECT

After your demonstration, your early learners should be ready to make cutouts for their first "1, 2, 3" books. Many of them already identified their favorite food for the final page of their first personalized storybook. Cutouts can represent everything from oranges to apples to cookies to scoops of ice cream. The regularity of the cutting is not important, but the counting is.

For each of your children, you want to make sure that the right number gets printed on each page, and that the correct number of items get pasted on the page. When you spend a minute with each pupil individually on this project, help the child form the numbers correctly. Then the child can read the counting book to you, to others in the class, and to the family at home.

Making a personalized counting book is a project that involves reading, writing, and arithmetic. This first "1, 2, 3" book is a project to build on. You want each pupil to keep on making additional personalized counting books until the reading and writing of the numbers becomes as automatic as the counting.

15

◆ ◆ ◆

Introduce More Numbers, Words, and Personalized Books

Overview

These are the topics you will meet in this chapter:

- How to Expand on the First Steps
- Individualizing the Areas of Expansion
- Higher Numbers in Counting Books
- Wordbanks for the Words That Pupils Request
- How to Teach Requested Words
- Personalizing Additional Storybooks

HOW TO EXPAND ON THE FIRST STEPS

Now that you and your child have taken the first steps into the 3 Rs, you will find that there are many different ways in which you can continue. Here are some expansions on the early steps.

- Help your pupil make counting books that feature numbers beyond 1, 2, and 3.
- Have each early reader or writer tell you what additional words he or she wants to learn.
- Present these child-selected words on wordcards for each individual's wordbank.

- Help with the writing of personalized storybooks where these words are used.

Individualizing the Areas of Expansion

Some pupils take the first steps into arithmetic quite comfortably, but they lag behind in writing or reading. Some make rapid strides in writing and enjoy reading to you whatever they write. Early learners are highly individualistic in their progress on the first steps into reading, writing, and arithmetic.

There is no need for a pupil to achieve total competence on the early first steps in all 3 Rs before progressing to these continuing steps. It's fine to go forward with reading only, or writing only, or arithmetic only, if that pattern fits the child. If your pupil enjoys playing phonics games and making "1, 2, 3" books, but does not retain words on wordcards, proceed with the games and the counting books, and slow down on your teaching of new words. If your child is an eager writer who likes to make copies of wordcards, but does not seem interested in numbers, follow the child's lead. Chances are that your pupil will catch up on arithmetic later.

If your child comes to a temporary standstill in reading, writing, or arithmetic, try some of the activities that are suggested in Unit III. Sometimes the novelty of a different approach is just what the child needs.

You should expect your pupils to reach leveling-off periods, or learning plateaus, frequently. So you can plan on going back and forth between Unit III and Unit II, intersperging new strategies with the activities suggested in the chapter.

HIGHER NUMBERS IN COUNTING BOOKS

The first "1, 2, 3" books were just the starting point for further progress into the early 3 Rs. Personalized counting books can blend arithmetic with vocabulary building and concept building.

Consider the simple cut-and-paste possibilities of counting books. Suppose you wanted to combine the making of a counting book with reinforcing the shape of a triangle. You could have a child paste one triangle on the "1" page, two triangles on the "2" page, three triangles on the "3" page, and four triangles on the "4" page. You could review the concepts of the square and the rectangle similarly.

Sometimes drawing is better learning activity than pasting. You could tell the preschool dinosaur enthusiast who wants to personalize a counting book of dinosaurs, to draw the right number of creatures on each page. If the child draws too many or too few, count them aloud with him, and correct the number. Counting books are tools for learning, so not every book will be perfect.

If pupils work at home on making counting books, you will get some interesting variations, especially when their parents decide to help. A little girl with long hair brought in one brush, two combs, three barrettes, and four ribbon bows in her book. The book had a bag pasted on each big cardboard page to hold the items. A lock of her hair was taped to the cover.

A little boy from a large family brought in a group photo that he had permission to cut apart in class—to show one sister, two brothers, three aunts, and four cousins in a personalized album.

One child who loved the story of Snow White made a counting book of the seven dwarfs. You can go as far with counting books as you think is advisable for your pupils.

Counting is very effectively reinforced at read-aloud time. You can share not only the types of counting books that contain few words (mostly pictures and numbers) but also the types that connect a story, poem, or song to the counting. Children's books feature everything from "Three Blind Mice" to "The Twelve Days of Christmas."

The folktale of Rapunzel's long hair can inspire a trip to the measuring center, for measuring ponytails, pigtails, and bangs—none of which come close to Rapunzel's ladder-long hair, that reached down from her prison tower to the ground. But a child-made counting book could feature yarn of one inch, two inches, three inches, and more, in imitation of hair. Read-aloud time can greatly enrich your teaching of the first steps into arithmetic.

WORDBANKS FOR THE WORDS
THAT PUPILS REQUEST

Your child's favorite food was featured at the end of the first personalized storybook that you made. It was also pictured in the child's first "1, 2, 3" book. So, when you ask a pupil if he or she would like to learn to read that word, the child's answer will probably be yes. Words for favorite foods like *apples, oranges,* and *cookies* are popular additions to wordbanks.

Other words that a child might request are the names of family and friends. You might also teach a few action verbs, suggested by the child. Every day or two, ask your pupil, "Whose name would you like to learn to read and write?" Or ask, "What do you like to do outdoors—run, jump, slide, climb? Which word should I print on a card for you?" Early readers pick up words they want to learn easily and rapidly. So be prepared with blank index cards and a box (wordbank) for each child.

Each time a name is requested, print it on a wordcard for the child's collection. Capitalize the first letter of each proper name, but use lower-case printing for the other letters. Don't capitalize the common nouns or the verbs. Each pupil will have an individual collection in his or her wordbank.

Usually names of family members, friends, and pets can be learned fairly easily, provided the words in print do not closely resemble each other. For example, for an early reader, the name *Rodney* could be confused with the name *Ricky*, because the names are somewhat similar in configuration, and they begin and end with the same letters. You would not give those two names to a child on the same day.

It's easy to review the namecards by having a pupil do any or all of these activities:

- Sort the namecards—girls in one pile and boys in another, or family in one pile and pets in another.
- Spread out all the cards, and hand you the one that you request.
- Match each card that you printed with a card that the child copied.
- Print some names on envelopes for your classroom mailcall.

Again, remember that every early learner is different, even in patterns of learning to read names. One pupil might read many namecards before attempting to write any name beyond his or her own. Another pupil might learn to read by writing, carefully printing each letter of each new name.

As always, follow the lead of the child, and proceed at that child's own pace. Some pupils want only one new name each week. Others ask you for an additional namecard every day. And still others copy your printing so well that they can make their own sets of namecards.

To introduce a few verbs, ask your pupil what he or she likes to do. Talk about whatever action interests the child. Get your pupil to demonstrate the action. Make a wordcard for the action verb. Hold up the card and have the child perform the action.

The verbs that have personal meaning for your pupil are the easiest ones for the child to learn. The word *swim*, for example, might be learned very quickly by a child who just learned to swim. The verbs *draw* and *paint* would probably be meaningful to a child who elects to spend lots of time at the easel. An affectionate child might want to read and write the word *hugs*. That verb is handy for making sentences with a proper noun before and after, such as "Mommy hugs Andrew" or "Daddy hugs Mommy."

How to Teach Requested Words

Let's consider how you would teach the name of a pet collie, *Rover*, and the action verb, *jumps*. Print *Rover* on a wordcard, as always using a capital letter for the first letter only. Hold up the wordcard and say to your pupil, "This is the word you said you wanted—*Rover*, the name of your dog." Have the child repeat the word while pointing to it on the wordcard.

Help the child read it in some sentences made with other word cards, such as "Mommy called Rover." For review the next day, have your child shuffle through his or her box of wordcards to find *Rover*.

When your pupil requests the action word *jumps*, have the child demonstrate jumping. Ask how the dog Rover jumps. How is Rover's jumping different from a child's jumping? Hold up the wordcard (printed in all lower-case let-ters—*jumps*) and say to your pupil:

> *This word is jumps. Say it with me —jumps.*
> *Your dog Rover jumps on you when you go home.*
> *Your friend Stefani jumps rope on the playground.*
> *Your baby brother jumps when you say "Boo."*
> *Now, let me hear you read this word.*

Mix the wordcard for *jumps* with the child's other wordcards. Arrange that when you hold up the wordcard *jumps*, your pupil will read the word aloud and jump. Praise the child for remembering. Repeat this procedure frequently for re-view.

If your early reader has learned to connect the initial consonant j with the sound /j/, use phonics in your presentation of the word *jumps*.

In the primary grades, your pupil will learn to read the forms *jump, jumped*, and *jumping*. But just one form of a word at the beginning seems best for most early learners, and the form *jumps* is handiest for use in sentences such as "Rover jumps."

Personalizing Additional Storybooks

Whenever you review wordcards with a child, you want to put them in sen-tences. These sentences can lead to additional personalized storybooks, based on personal incidents.

Suppose, for example, that Linda, the child who requested the name of her dog *Rover*, asked also for a wordcard for the neighbor's dog, *Fido*. She wanted the words *bit* and *cried* too because Fido was constantly getting into dog fights with Rover and biting him. Then, one day, Fido bit Linda herself, and Rover came to her rescue.

Linda might tell you a long version of the incident at show-and-tell time. But for a personalized storybook, you could boil the incident down to four sen-tences, composed of words Linda can already read.

> Fido bit Linda.
> Linda cried.
> Rover bit Fido.
> Fido cried.

It is best to use words from the child's own wordbank when you compose per-sonalized stories. If there are many unfamiliar words, even the familiar context can not keep the beginner from getting frustrated. Occasionally, an early reader can figure out one new word from the context among a lot of familiar words. Your pupils will enjoy their personalized storybooks more if you make them as easy as possible to read.

Some children want to write their own stories, and others prefer to dictate to you and have you do the writing. When you print words in a personalized storybook, use capital and lower-case letters to make the words appear just as they would in a regular book. If you are leaving room for illustrations or photos, print only one sentence per page.

Keep your sentences very short. Two-word sentences do the whole job in a "Carolina" book containing pictures of her in action on the sliding board:

Carolina climbs.
Carolina slides.
Carolina laughs.

Two-word sentences are all you need for a "pool" book for Mackenzie:

Mackenzie splashes.
Mackenzie jumps.
Mackenzie swims.

Fancy covers are not necessary. A personalized storybook for an early reader can be just a piece of paper folded in half with a sentence on each page. If you and your pupil want to be a little fancier, you can staple together a few sheets of paper on which you and the child have printed the sentences. Then, there is more room for the child to draw illustrations or to paste suitable photos in the book.

When your pupil reads the storybook to you, point to each word and move your hand from left to right under the line of print. This helps the child internalize directionality in reading. Your pointing also helps the child keep in place and move smoothly from one word to the next. Keep all your early readers imitating your intonation patterns so that they group words meaningfully as they read.

Encourage your early readers to be writers, too. Not only can they copy your sentences, but they can also try to print their own original stories, using their boxes of wordcards as wordbanks for writing. As they compose, they may come to you for additional words that they want to use in their stories. Frequent rereading of their personalized storybooks is an excellent way for your pupils to review their words and strengthen their reading abilities.

Young children will greatly enjoy their early first steps into the 3 Rs if you help them make counting books on topics that interest them, and if you teach them the words they request. Then, they can practice reading and writing those words in sentences in personalized storybooks. Your early 3 Rs program is not only instructional, but also fun for your pupils.

16

◆ ◆ ◆

Use Child-Selected
Words for Teaching
More Phonics

> *Overview*
>
> These are the topics you will meet in this chapter:
>
> • Letter-Sound Relationships of Initial Consonants
> • Consonant and Vowel Considerations
> • Phonics in Early Writing and Spelling
> • Combining Context With Phonics

LETTER-SOUND RELATIONSHIPS
OF INITIAL CONSONANTS

Your early readers took their first steps into phonics by learning the letter-sound relationships of M as in *Mommy*, c as in *called*, and the initial letters of their names and yours. Now you can use the additional words they requested to teach them more letter-sound relationships. The initial letters of self-selected words are a child's best reference points for further steps into phonics.

Consider the child named Linda (from the dogbite story in the preceding chapter). Among the words she requested, in addition to *Rover* and *jumps*, were *bit, Fido, teeth,* and *Grandma.* Let's list those words, and see what additional letter-sound relationships you could teach from the initial consonant in each of them.

bit	b
Fido	F
Grandma	G
jumps	j
Rover	R
teeth	t

Your personalized phonics lessons for Linda would be based on the initial letters and sounds of words she requested for her wordbank.

You would make a grid for Linda with her six familiar letters on it. With her, it would be easy to talk about the sound /b/ as in *bit*, the sound /f/ as in *Fido*, etc. You could have her point to and name letters on the grid as she answers the questions below.

b	F	G
j	R	t

- Which letter stands for the sound /j/ as in jumps?
- What is the name of the letter that Fido starts with? What is the sound of that letter?
- Point to the letter that Rover starts with, the letter that says /r/.
- You can read the word teeth. What sound do you hear at the beginning of that word? What letter do you see?
- Name and make the sound of the first letter in the word Grandma. Find that letter on the grid.
- You know the letter and sound that bit starts with. What letter and sound do you think the word bite starts with? Name and point to that letter.

It is worth the trouble to individualize and personize your early teaching of phonics because it's important for a beginner to have a familiar word to "hang onto" as the child connects its initial letter with a sound. Sounds are more abstract than words. Associating a sound with the first letter of a familiar word helps an early learner.

CONSONANT AND VOWEL CONSIDERATIONS

As a general rule, consonant sounds are easier for beginners than vowel sounds, so you usually want to teach consonant sounds first. But if a child's name begins with a vowel, or if the name of a favorite friend, relative, or pet begins with a vowel, the child will probably learn to associate the vowel sound with the initial letter because of the close connection.

When you make a 6-letter grid from the child's wordcard collection, you will probably want to choose a majority of initial consonants. If you include vowels, try to limit them to one or two per grid. At this early stage in phonics, some teachers help children learn the common sounds of six initial consonants from words they recognize, and leave all vowel sounds until later, and that's fine.

If a pupil is quick at learning to read words by sight from wordcards, the child may need to make only minimal use of phonics. It is best to teach early readers to combine phonics and context, and thereby figure out new words by sound and sense.

Phonics in Early Writing and Spelling

Some early learners want to write, so they use whatever they've learned about letter names and letter sounds in their efforts to spell words. Some of their stories are hard for an adult to read because one or two letters may represent a whole word.

These stories, however, are well worth saving over a period of months because you can really see progress. In fall, a child might "spell" dinosaur with a barely legible D and a squiggle. In winter, the D might be followed by an N and an S. By spring, the child might insist on your helping with the correct spelling of the whole word.

Whenever an early writer asks you how to spell a phonetically regular word, you have an opportunity for a quick phonics lesson. You can reply:

> Let's say that word together. What sound
> do you hear at the beginning of the word?
> What is the letter for that sound?
> What other sounds do you hear in that word?
> What are the letters for those sounds?

Of course, many frequently used words do not yield to phonics. Your early writers need direct help from you with those words, especially with the vowels in the middles of such words. But phonics is usually helpful, at least with the consonant at the beginning of a word.

Combining Context With Phonics

Phonics is a valuable tool for decoding words, but it is not the only tool that early readers need. They need to make good use of picture clues, configuration clues, and context clues. Awareness of context is especially important.

An unfamiliar word must make sense in a sentence. Suppose Linda, for example, encountered the sentence, "Rover eats dog biscuits." Suppose she knew the first three words by sight from wordcards, but the word *biscuits* was unfamiliar to her in print. (Of course, she had heard and spoken the word, so she knew it orally.)

Sounding out the whole word *biscuits* would be too much to expect of a beginner. But Linda could look at the initial letter b, associate it with the sound /b/, and consider the context of the sentence. What does Rover eat that starts with the letter b and fits at the end of the sentence, "Rover eats dog b———"? The possibilities that spring to mind are *bones* and *biscuits*, and *biscuits* is the better choice, in terms of both phonetics and semantics. This type of reasoning is similar to the thinking of adults who work crossword puzzles. Early readers use an elementary form of such reasoning when they combine phonics with context to figure out an unfamiliar word.

It's never too soon to lead a child toward using phonics and context together. Readers continue to combine those word-recognition tools all through their lives.

17

◆ ◆ ◆

Summary of Unit II

HOW TO HELP EARLY LEARNERS
TAKE THEIR FIRST STEPS INTO THE 3 Rs

For early learners who are well prepared, the first steps into reading, writing, and arithmetic are enjoyable and rewarding. In just minutes a day, you can individualize and personalize your instruction to help each child progress at his or her individual pace through these first steps into early learning of the 3 Rs.

Teach Each Beginning Reader Four Words

Each child who can benefit from early reading instruction will learn to recognize these four words: (a) his or her own first name, (b) the word *Mommy*, (c) the word *called*, and (d) your name. The child can also learn to read these four words in sentences.

Help Each Child Write a Personalized Storybook

You can make an author out of each child who helps with the writing of a personalized book. By using just the words that he or she can recognize from wordcards, the child can create an easy-to-read story that features a personal choice treat.

Connect Familiar Initial Letters With Their Sounds

The words on each child's four wordcards are the instructional materials for your first steps in phonics. These words are familiar. With your excellent teaching, each child has a good chance at learning the letter-sound relationships of the initial letters of these words.

Make a Personalized "1, 2, 3" Book With Each Early Learner

A personalized counting book is as effective for early arithmetic as a personalized storybook is for early reading and writing. A child who has internalized the concepts of one, two, and three can take the first steps into arithmetic by writing the numbers and making a counting book that he or she can read.

Introduce More Numbers, Words, and Personalized Books

A young child can most easily learn self-selected names and action verbs. So, make wordcards for whatever nouns and verbs the child requests. Your pupil can then read and write storybooks where those words appear. You also want to help the child make additional counting books.

Use Child-Selected Words for Teaching More Phonics

To go forward in phonics, your pupil can most easily learn the letter-sound relationships that are connected with initial letters of familiar, self-selected words. Therefore, you want to teach individualized, personalized phonics from the words each child requests.

Unit III

◆ ◆ ◆

How to Expand and Vary Strategies for Early Teaching of the 3 Rs

18

♦ ♦ ♦

Preview of Unit III: Expand Strategies for Early Teaching

Some children take the early first steps into the 3 Rs in nursery school or right at the beginning of kindergarten. They soon need variations on the teaching tools described up to this point (wordcards, phonics games, personalized storybooks, and counting books). Variations in your teaching strategies will help your fast-moving early learners to progress further in reading, writing, and arithmetic.

When you were teaching the first few words, you regularly used wordcards as your main instructional materials. When you were teaching the first few letter-sound relationships in phonics, you repeatedly used the method of emphasizing initial sounds. For sentence practice, you used personalized storybooks again and again. For the first steps into early arithmetic, you used counting books repeatedly, with higher and higher numbers featured in the books. You individualized and personalized most of your instruction, trying to give each early learner one-to-one attention for a minute or two a day.

For those children who have comfortably taken the first steps into reading, writing, or arithmetic, it's time to expand your methods and vary your materials. It is also time to offer some of your 3 Rs instruction to groups or even to the whole class, rather than just to individuals, although you will have to maintain one-on-one times with those children who still need personalization.

Let's consider what to do and why to do it in terms of a variety of new instructional strategies.

WHAT TO DO

To broaden the early learning of the 3 Rs for a young child, and to intensify the child's interest in reading, writing, and arithmetic you can employ the following approaches:

- Use software and equipment to enrich your teaching
- Move toward math operations with children's books
- Start a word wall of pupils' names in alphabetical order
- Go beyond concrete nouns and action verbs
- Teach the whole alphabet for reading, writing, and phonics
- Stimulate new areas of language development

There is no prescribed best order for these approaches. Pick and choose among them according to your children's interests and abilities.

The math-focused software programs and children's books in chapters 19 and 20 help early learners with arithmetic, but some of them also promote reading and writing. No doubt your children will make good use of your edu-taining CD-ROMs all year, so these disks can be introduced to your pupils at any time, even when you are still working on the first steps in the 3 Rs from Unit II.

You may want to move immediately into the word wall activities in chapter 21, that begin with the easiest words, the names of all your pupils. Then you can try the special strategies in chapter 22 for introducing more difficult words.

Or, if you are already focusing on the whole alphabet and are teaching letter names and letter sounds every day, chapter 23 might be a good starting point in Unit III. Read the whole unit and see what strategies fit best in the early 3 Rs program you are developing with your pupils.

As you continue to read aloud to your children every day, to converse in arithme-talk and count with them, and help them develop fluency in their speaking and writing as suggested in chapter 24, you will no doubt be using many of the strategies from Unit III simultaneously.

WHY TO DO IT

Though some children stay happily occupied with personalized storybooks and counting books all through nursery school, kindergarten, and even beyond, other children crave the stimulation provided by new approaches.

In one day, a young child may want to play a phonics game, recite a nursery rhyme, sign a get-well card to a classmate, hear you read a favorite story aloud, view a videotape of that same story, count wordcards, talk with you about the birth of a litter of puppies, and tape record a counting story about the litter. This is an eclectic set of activities, but all of them promote literacy.

All these activities fit the eclectic approach to early instruction in the 3 Rs, because this approach includes a little bit of everything. The eclectic approach encourages you to use a wide variety of developmentally appropriate teaching techniques to stimulate your early learners.

The techniques from the preceding chapters helped your children take the first steps in the 3 Rs. Those techniques offered the easiest ways to begin, and they will continue to be the foundations from which the new strategies spring. But once a child has mastered the first steps in reading, writing, or arithmetic, it's time make your program more eclectic. You now need multiple methods and materials, a big bag of tricks, perhaps something different for each early learner in your class.

Today's authorities agree that there is no one way to teach reading, writing, or arithmetic that is best for all pupils. In light of this agreement, there should be more eclectic instruction in all preschool and primary classes.

Reading instruction experts used to be divided into many camps, each favoring one method, such as phonics, look-say, whole-language, or literature-based reading. The authorities of today say that a reading instruction program should draw from all methods.

From the start of your 3 Rs program, your early reading instruction strategies have included phonemic awareness and the phonics of letter-sound relationships, the look-say of environmental print and wordcards, and the whole-language literature-based emphasis of a daily read-aloud time. So you have provided a balanced approach to reading in your early 3 Rs program.

There was a time when writing instruction experts stressed perfection of the mechanics, from penmanship to spelling to punctuation. Now the reading–writing connection starts in preschool, so perfecting the mechanics comes later. Even in primary classes, the main emphasis is on effectiveness of written communication.

Whether you favor emphasizing mathematical concepts, problem-solving, or operations, your pupils need to deal with all three in early arithmetic. In your early 3 Rs program, your activities have already included arithme-talk about quantity concepts, the solving of problems of distribution at snack time, and counting (toward the operations of mathematics).

The chapters in this unit will get you started on some age-appropriate strategies for broadening and varying your early teaching of the 3 Rs. As always, you need to remember that young children progress in irregular patterns as they begin to learn reading, writing, and arithmetic. Often they seem to stop progressing in one area, and move forward on another front. Very few progress charts show a diagonal line going steadily upward. For most children, the line on the progress chart zigzags up and down, with frequent plateaus, or *leveling-off periods*.

Leveling-off periods can raise questions in the minds of teachers of young children, such as is it advisable to review, or drop all early instruction for a while, or try new methods and materials?

If a child is showing little interest in reviewing and rereading personalized storybooks, there is not much point in pushing those books. So, reviewing only is not an advisable option.

Dropping all early instruction is too extreme. After all, the child mastered enough of the early first steps to make some personalized books. That is ample evidence that the pupil can continue to progress on some front. With your guidance, the child might start to apply counting to inches on a yardstick, or might even progress further by some method that differs a bit from the personalized counting book strategy.

A new teaching strategy will often trigger a new spurt of progress in reading, writing, or arithmetic, so the best option during a leveling-off period is to try new methods and materials.

The strategies in the following chapters spring from the starting points of wordcards, phonics games, personalized storybooks, and counting books. They are variations on those original themes. You need variations and alternate strategies, because your pupils present you with pauses, leveling-off periods, and learning plateaus, as well as spurts of speedy progress. These strategies are useful not only with preschoolers but also with primary pupils whose progress charts are showing a flat-line period.

As you move forward in offering early instruction in the 3 Rs using an eclectic approach, the activities in the next unit will give you a variety of ways to help your pupils.

19

◆ ◆ ◆

Use Software
and Equipment to Enrich
Your Teaching

Overview

These are the topics you will meet in this chapter:

- From Expensive to Inexpensive
- Making Audiotapes
- Learning to Read Words from Audiotapes
- Headsets for Listening to Stories
- Videotapes and Books: Comparing and Contrasting
- Teaching the Handling of Hardware and Software
- Choosing and Using CD-ROMs
- Your First Round With a New CD-ROM
- Rediscovering Simple Equipment

FROM EXPENSIVE TO INEXPENSIVE

From tapes to television to telecommunications on the Internet, electronic equipment can enrich your teaching. You can make good use of everything from simple toys to complex computers, and it is wonderful to teach with a generous budget for equipment. But your school may not be able to afford much. Many schools have a hard time just keeping supplies on hand.

If your school's budget is very tight, there is one piece of equipment you can still afford, even if you have to supply it yourself. It is a tape recorder. Just insert a blank audiotape cassette into an inexpensive tape recorder, and you are set to provide a child with a new literacy experience.

Making Audiotapes

Suppose that you have read "The Little Red Hen" to your pupils repeatedly and have thoroughly discussed the story and its illustrations. Suppose one little girl is so fond of the story that she has memorized parts of it, and can tell you when to turn each page.

Your next step with that child might be to have her tape-record her "reading" of the story. You and she can get a lot of educational mileage out of her audiotaping. When a child tape-records her version of a story, she is giving evidence of her comprehension. She may start with "Once upon a time," showing that she knows the traditional folktale opener. She may follow the general sequence of events, but skip some incidents and elaborate on her favorite parts.

With any retelling, your pupil is exercising language development. But on an audiotaped retelling, you have captured the child's exact words that you can put on paper for her. You may have to divide her flow of words into sentences, and delete a few "and uhs," but the tape-recorded sentences are sentences she may be able to learn to read.

Learning to Read Words From Audiotapes

Take one short sentence from your child's audiotaped story and print it on a sheet of paper. Have her copy her sentence, or draw a picture to go with it. Praise the child's work when she is finished.

Even if she does not care to write or draw, you can still read her sentence to her, pointing at each word as you read. Then ask her to help you with just one of her words, perhaps a concrete noun or an action verb. If she can name the word, cheer, clap, and tell her she is a great reader. Help her trace that word with her finger.

Replay the audiotape that she made, so that she hears her own voice saying the sentence you printed on paper, saying the very word that she is now reading.

Repeat the whole procedure the next day. If she remembers the word she read, try the process on another word from the same short sentence.

If your pupil learns a second and third word from the sentence you printed, take out another piece of paper and print the sentence again. Show the child that it is the same sentence.

Then cut the sentence apart, so that each word is separate. After that, demonstrate matching. Compare the first word you cut apart from the sentence with the first word in the complete sentence. They match, so place one word on top of the other. After you demonstrate this matching for each word, have your pupil try to do it.

Reread the sentence aloud. Ask your pupil to read it with you. She probably will not be able to remember all the words, but she may retain the two or three you taught her from the audiotape. She can add those words to her wordbank, along with all the words she learned from the wordcard method.

Note, however, that she learned these new words in a different way. Rather than starting with a wordcard, she started with a whole story that she told on an audiotape. From the story, you and she used the *top-down* approach. Together, you proceeded from the story to a sentence to a word. This strategy is different from the method used in the original first steps into the 3 Rs.

Headsets for Listening to Stories

Often the children who want to tape-record their retellings of their favorite stories are good listeners as well as good speakers. They may have built their listening skills, as well as their familiarity with a particular story, while wearing headsets at your listening center.

Headsets are familiar equipment in early childhood classrooms. They promote silence at the listening station since the children get absorbed in the stories they are hearing. For very young children you must insert and remove tapes and turn the equipment on and off. But most kindergarteners can learn to operate the simple equipment themselves.

Audiotapes of popular children's books will give your pupils many hours of happy listening. Some early learners consider listening time with headsets almost as enjoyable as read-aloud time.

You can get book-and-tape sets for beginners from most libraries. Any pupil who loves a particular story and wants to hear it again and again will keep returning to the tape and its accompanying book. Professionally made tapes often provide musical background for stories and tone-signals to show a listener when to turn the page. But if no commercial tape is available for a book that is a favorite with your pupils, why not tape-record it yourself? Your children will enjoy hearing the story in their own teacher's voice.

VIDEOTAPES AND BOOKS:
COMPARING AND CONTRASTING

As a teacher of young children, you can usually count on having access to a VCR with a monitor. You may want to use this equipment to show videotapes of classics like Pinocchio, Cinderella, and Peter Pan after you have read the stories aloud. Children today are often introduced to these stories on the monitor at home before they hear the tales read aloud from books.

The books and videotapes can enrich each other. The two media enable children to compare and contrast different versions of the classics. So you may want to enrich your read-aloud times with the video versions of famous tales. Then you can ask:

> — *How were the book and video different?*
> — *What parts of the story were the same in the book and in the video?*

Of course, famous old tales bring pleasure to children with the simple equipment of puppetry (a stage with curtains, or an overhead projector for shadow puppets). Because many of your pupils may have seen videotapes at home, they may be more thrilled with your "new equipment" of a puppet stage than the "old stuff" of a videotape.

TEACHING THE HANDLING OF HARDWARE AND SOFTWARE

If you have one or more computers in your classroom, you want to set them up in a child-friendly manner. Safety first, of course. Do you have a surge-protector power strip with multiple outlets? If so, have you blocked any unused outlets with safety plugs? Have you bundled the wires behind the computer with twist-ties, to get them out of the way?

These precautions are basic. But the most protective precaution of all is to talk, talk, talk to your children, both in groups and individually, about how to treat computers and CD-ROMs. Use the word "gently" many times. Some teachers actually personify the equipment: they talk about how much it hurts the mouse to be dropped on the floor.

Just as you teach the skills of book handling, you want to teach children the skills of CD-ROM handling. These disks are durable, but not indestructible. If the shiny aluminum coating on the bottom is scratched or damaged, the disk won't work.

Children's hands are not big enough to grasp a CD-ROM the adult way, in one hand with fingers and thumb touching only the rim. Children need to use both hands. So, when you demonstrate proper CD handling to your pupils, you might say:

> *See how I use both hands to hold the CD at the rim.*
> *Now see how I place the disk in the tray, gently,*
> *shiny side down. I make sure that it is flat in*
> *the tray. Then, it can slide into the CD-ROM drive,*
> *and we can start to play it.*

Choosing and Using CD-ROMs

The pages of many popular books for children are embellished with hotspots on the CD-ROM versions of these books. Often you get the storybook in the same box with the CD-ROM. After your early learners have clicked on every hotspot, seen the animation of each background object, and heard the story aloud repeatedly at the computer, they often return to the book, and quietly enjoy just turning the pages. They are then able to follow the story and "read" at least the pictures if not all the words.

Some of today's edu-taining CD-ROMs, however, go far beyond just recreating a story with animated embellishments. The disks are well designed instructional systems. They do a good job of teaching letter and number recognition, counting, and phonics, often using characters from famous stories.

Characters like Madeline, Curious George, and Mogli have lasting appeal, generation after generation. They charm the children of today, perhaps even more than they charmed the children of years past. In the past youngsters met these characters only in books, but today they also meet them on the computer. Some interactive CD-ROMs use such characters to help early learners with the 3 Rs. The computer programs enable children to play their way into reading, writing, and arithmetic.

Though classic characters abound on CD-ROMs, it is hard to predict what programs will earn classic status. The programs are too new to have stood the test of time. Also, publishers of CDs frequently revise and upgrade their disks as technology improves.

Certain series, however, have established award-winning records, and include disks especially designed for kindergarten and prekindergarten children. The disks are usually labeled with suggested ages or grade levels. You might want to view the CD-ROMs from some of these series:

- Alphabet Express (School Zone)
- Dr. Seuss Learning Systems (Broderbund)
- Elmo's Reading: Preschool and Kindergarten (Creative Wonders Sesame Street Series)
- Jumpstart Series (Knowledge Adventure)
- Math Blaster (Davidson)
- Millie and Bailey (Edmark)
- Reader Rabbit (The Learning Company)
- Thinkin' Things (Edmark)
- Winnie the Pooh, and other Disney classics (Disney Interactive)

For reviews of software for early learners, you can consult the Children's Software Revue on the Internet at: www.childrenssoftware.com. From this Web site you can travel to the Publishers Directory and the Children's Software Finder for more information.

Your First Round With a New CD-ROM

Loading software can be tricky, so it's a good idea to try out your new CD-ROM by yourself before you use it with your children. You want to install the program ahead of time to be sure it will work on your computer. The instruction booklets that come with CD-ROMs for early learners have good suggestions for the adults who will guide the children through the activities. They are well worth reading.

Because disks are labeled for "Ages 2–4" or "Ages 5–7" or "Ages 2–5" (quite a spread), you need to preview the activities and decide which ones are suitable for each of your children. They may not be able to figure out how to get from one level to another, so you need to know all the secrets of a program.

Young children appear to have longer attention spans at the computer when they are working in groups of two or three, helping each other. After you have launched a small group of early learners on a new CD-ROM, you can often depend on their staying with the program and learning from it independently while you work with other pupils.

REDISCOVERING SIMPLE EQUIPMENT

The term *educational equipment* seems to conjure up visions of the latest model computer with the flashiest software, or the newest kit of manipulatives. But sometimes, for young children, the simplest equipment is the best.

Along with audiotapes, headsets, videotapes, computers, and software, remember all the simple pieces of equipment in your measuring center, such as tape measures and scales. Monthly measurements of height and weight can help your pupils keep track of their growth in inches and pounds. Using only this very basic equipment, you provide regular reinforcements for a child's interest in early arithmetic.

20

♦ ♦ ♦

Move Toward Math
Through Children's Books

Overview

These are the topics you will meet in this chapter:

• Arithme-talk About Books That Focus on Math
• Addition and Subtraction Connections
• Multiplication and Division Connections
• Stories of Telling Time, Measuring, and Sorting
• The Math–Literature Connection

ARITHME-TALK ABOUT BOOKS
THAT FOCUS ON MATH

You know from experience how much arithme-talk you can generate at read-aloud time. You are well aware of the effectiveness of counting books in fostering the mathematical growth of early learners. Other math-focused books can help your children move toward the operations of arithmetic.

Although the operations of addition, subtraction, multiplication and division are not formally taught until the primary grades, they are presented with great simplicity in some books for early learners.

Addition and Subtraction Connections

For the addition connection, consider *Annie's One to Ten* by Annie Owen (Knopf). This is more than a counting book because it shows combinations of numbers that can add up to ten (e.g., five birthday cakes and five ice cream cones, or nine clouds and one rainbow).

Another book that suggests addition through its illustrations is Susi Bohdal's *1, 2, 3. What Do You See?* (North-South Books). On the page showing five camels, for example, the main illustration shows all the camels together, although two are brown and three are tan. The smaller illustration on the bottom border shows another way to make five: one camel alone and two pairs of two camels each.

The book, *26 Letters and 99 Cents* by Tana Hoban (Greenwillow Books) features numbers as represented by pennies, nickels, dimes, quarters, so it leads into the addition of money.

For the subtraction connection, consider *Ten Bears in My Bed* by Stan Mack (Pantheon). In this countdown book, the bears are subtracted one by one, as they leave the little boy's bed. *A Bag Full of Pups* by Dick Gackenbach (Tichnor and Fields) is a story about giving away puppies. Your pupils can keep tallying the number that are left as each pup gets a home.

In *Six Sandy Sheep* (Boyds Mills Press) by Judith Enderle and Stephanie Tessler, alliteration and tongue twisters are thrown in for good measure, but the focus of this book in on subtraction. The text and pictures clearly show that six sheep minus one equals five; five minus one equals four; four minus one equals three, and on down. *Ten Apples Up on Top* by Theo LeSieg (Random House) shows subtraction as difference, when the animals who are balancing apples on their heads drop some.

Multiplication and Division Connections

For the multiplication connection, consider *One Wide River to Cross* by Barbara Emberly (Prentice-Hall). In this rhyming book the animals come to Noah's ark, two by two, three by three, four by four, up to ten. The text and pictures help young children begin counting by 2s, 3s, and 4s, a form of preparation for multiplication. Also consider Joy Hulme's book, *Sea Squares* (Hyperion Books). Hulme writes about sea creatures, such as 4 seals with 16 flippery feet.

You can adapt many counting books toward the thinking behind multiplication at read-aloud time. But you need to ask different types of questions to match the different abilities of your pupils. For example, if the "3" page shows three puppies, and one of your listeners is still struggling with one-to-one correspondence, you can use the old strategy of having that child count and touch each puppy. However, if another of your listeners needs more challenging questions, you can use a new strategy and lead into the thinking behind multiplication by saying to that child:

Three puppies—how many ears?
Three puppies—how many legs?

Three puppies—how many eyes?
Three puppies—how many tails?

In Joseph Slate's recent book, *Miss Bindergarten Celebrates the 100th Day of Kindergarten* (Dutton Children's Books), each child in alphabetical order must bring "100 of some wonderful, one-hundred-full thing." The pupils respond with 100 seeds, 100 beads, 100 raspberry tarts, and 100 candy hearts. Celebrations of 100 days in kindergarten have become increasingly popular and have spread across the country. This book and the 100th day celebrations promote counting by ones and tens up to 100.

For the division connection, consider Pat Hutchins' book, *The Doorbell Rang* (Morrow Publishers). In this story, Victoria and Sam have to share their cookies with friends who come visiting. Each time an additional child arrives at the door, they divide the cookies still another time. The story takes Victoria and Sam from six cookies each down to one cookie each, as the doorbell keeps ringing and more friends keep joining them at the table. Then, however, Grandma arrives with more cookies, so all is well.

For an animal version of the same division idea, consider Louise Mathews' book, *Gator Pie* (Dodd Mead). The alligators, Alice and Alvin, want to divide a pie in half to eat, but other alligators keep coming. Soon they have cut the pie into 100 pieces. But the pieces are not even, so the alligators start fighting. Alice and Alvin, however, cleverly end up with half a pie each.

Stories of Telling Time, Measuring, Sorting

Clocks with moveable hands are abundant in early childhood classrooms. But children need to make a lot of connections before they can tell time. They need to recognize numerals, to grasp the concepts of minute and hour, and to understand the significance of each hand on the clock. Telling time is not easy, but these books might help.

Bruce McMillan's book, *Time to ...* (Lothrop) uses photos to show what a kindergartener does each hour of the day. The hours are featured also in *The Grouchy Ladybug* by Eric Carle (Harper). The ladybug challenges a different opponent, and then backs down, each hour of the day.

Your measuring center has helped your pupils begin to understand inches and feet, so they might enjoy some read-alouds that deal with these measurements. The inchworm in Lio Lionni's book, *Inch by Inch* (Astor-Honor) measures the flamingo's neck, the robin's tail, and the legs, beak, and body of other birds, and thereby, escapes being eaten. Rolf Myller's book, *How Big Is a Foot?* (Atheneum), shows the perils of literally measuring by a foot, when the king's carpenter measures by the length of his foot rather than the king's foot.

Nancy Carlson created a heroine who sorts candy by color, size, and favorites in *Harriet's Halloween Candy* (Puffin). In the story "A Lost Button" in *Frog and*

Toad are Friends by Arnold Lobel (Harper), Toad loses a button from his jacket. The sorting and classifying activities in the book can lead to similar activities with buttons in your classroom.

THE MATH–LITERATURE CONNECTION

Children love stories. Today's storybooks are beautifully and meaningfully illustrated, so they give a child both language and art. The aforementioned storybooks intertwine arithmetic in their plots, so they support all 3 Rs.

When a math concept is embedded in a story, it gains context. The math concept therefore becomes easier to understand. That is why connecting math and literature at read-aloud time gives a special boost to the arithmetic segment of your early 3 Rs program.

21

◆ ◆ ◆

Start a Word Wall of Pupils' Names in Alphabetical Order

Overview

These are the topics you will meet in this chapter:

• From Many Wordbanks to One Word Wall
• The Alphabet Song for Sequence of Letters
• A Word Wall Day for Each Child
• Size and Backing for Your Word Wall

FROM MANY WORDBANKS TO ONE WORD WALL

A word wall is a display area for groups of words that the class wants to read and write. Only after the whole class has talked about a word, read it, and written it can it be placed on the word wall.

The first names of the children in your class are the first group of words that you want to post in alphabetical order on your word wall, one name per day. Because every young child wants to "go first," the alphabet serves as a good way of establishing order without hurting feelings. Also, your word wall helps with the teaching of alphabetical order.

Even if you have two children in your class whose names start with the same letter (Patrick and Pedro), the word wall rule is still one name per day. A child's word wall day should be special. It's the day that every classmate sings about the child's name, reads it, and writes it. The child gets to wear a placard and a crown that shows the name on the front and back.

Each of your early learners already has an individual wordbank of self-selected words. The word wall is a class wordbank. Probably some of your pupils have already requested the names of their special friends for their individual wordbanks. Now you are promoting special attention for every name in the class on the word wall.

Anthony enjoys having his name featured first. Yolanda, at the far end of the alphabet, eagerly awaits her word wall day. Twins Eugene and Eula like separate days of attention for each of their names.

The Alphabet Song for Sequence of Letters

Your pupils need to be aware of the sequence of letters in the alphabet before you start posting their names on the word wall. Most of them have started to learn this sequence from the Alphabet Song. But even if they have memorized the song and sing it well, some of them do not associate each letter name with its printed symbol. Beginners often run "l, m, n, o, p" together, as if the five letters were one.

Encourage each pupil to sing the Alphabet Song slowly and to point at each letter while singing, in much the same way that a child touched each object while counting to establish one-to-one correspondence. A chart of model letters is handy for this activity.

In preparation for your word wall alphabetizing, print the A, B, Cs at the top of your chalkboard and have the children stand below their initials. Then say such things as:

> *If your name starts with A, sit on the floor.*
> *If your name starts with Y, jump twice.*
> *If your name starts with M, touch your nose.*
> *What letter does your name start with, Helen?*
> *What letter does Candy's name start with?*
> *Who else's name starts with Smoky's letter, S?*
> *Do we have anyone in class whose name starts with X?*
> *What letter is the first letter in the alphabet?*
> *What is the second letter of the alphabet?*
> *What is the last letter in the alphabet?*

These types of directions and questions call the children's attention to alphabetical order and to initial letters in names. Repeat the alphabet lineup daily so that each child becomes quick to take the proper position under his or her initial letter.

Try the Alphabet Song with each pupil singing his or her letter. You can sing in on the letters for which you have no pupils.

When you sit with a child who can recite the alphabet well, pointing at each letter in turn, try some "after" questions.

> — *What letter comes after A?*
> — *What is the next letter after D on the*
>   *alphabet chart?*
> — *What letter do you see after your initial?*

These alphabet activities will get your students prepared for starting a word wall on which their names are posted in alphabetical order.

A WORD WALL DAY FOR EACH CHILD

When it is Janet's word wall day, she arrives all smiles. You start by crowning her with her name. If you make one fancy cardboard crown, you can clip a different name to the front and back of it each day. The name attachments should be in very large print so that they can be seen across the room.

The class sings "Happy word wall day to you" to Janet, to the tune of "Happy birthday to you." You are then ready to print Janet's name on the chalkboard, naming each letter as you form it.

> *Janet's name starts with a capital J.*
> *Watch how I print the capital J, so that*
> *you can make your J look just like mine.*

(Demonstrate, and continue.)

> *Now, each of you should print a J for Janet.*

This can also be an opportunity for a phonics lesson that associates the letter J with the sound /j/. You may want to focus more on the writing than the phonics, since you'll be walking around, observing and helping your pupils with their printing.

Each of Janet's classmates tries to form the capital letter J on paper. Then you use the same procedures to help them print the lower-case letters in Janet's name. As you demonstrate the formation of the lower-case letters, your pupils keep trying to follow your lead. After all, this is Janet's word wall day, and she gets a gift from each classmate. The gift is her name, in the best writing each classmate can do.

You will collect the papers and hand them to Janet. Of course, they will vary greatly, with some friends signing their names, some drawing pictures around Janet's name, and some poking holes in the paper as they tried to form letters. It is wise to teach in advance that the word wall child should say a polite "Thank you" to all classmates no matter what the printing looks like.

The official posting of Janet's name on the word wall deserves a drum roll. Some teachers like to use large computer print, rather than their own personal printing, for each name, and later for other words that will be posted on the word wall.

Size and Backing for Your Word Wall

Maybe you want sheets of brick-patterned wallpaper for your word wall. Or maybe you want something as simple as a bulletin board. But when you decide on the size and the backing, plan ahead.

The names of your pupils are the first group of words you will post on your word wall. But there may be other groups of words that you want to present to the whole class for reading and writing. Perhaps some nouns and verbs that are already in quite a few individual wordbanks? Perhaps the days of the week? Perhaps a few high-frequency words? Only you can decide what words, how many, and what display system for the words is best for your early learners.

22

◆　◆　◆

Go Beyond
Concrete Nouns
and Action Verbs

Overview

These are the topics you will meet in this chapter:

- Frequently Used Words
- Testing the Water With "No" and "Yes"
- Getting Active With "Down" and "Up"
- Concept Books on Opposites
- Noting Degrees of Success

FREQUENTLY USED WORDS

Until now, most of the child-selected words you have presented have probably been nouns and verbs. The short, easy-to-read personalized books you've written for your early readers have contained mainly names and action words.

It is likely that some of your early learners are becoming capable of moving a step beyond noun and verb stories. Those pupils may be able to learn to read words like *no, yes, down,* and *up,* if you teach the words in ways that are developmentally appropriate for young children. These words are not as concrete as those you have taught up to this point, however. So you need some different teaching strategies.

Testing the Water With "No" and "Yes"

Your early readers are not likely to request the word *no* on a wordcard. It is probably not a word they feel eager to learn. But it is a good word for testing the waters on their capability for going beyond the self-selected nouns and verbs in their wordbanks.

The word *no* is familiar to young children. Your pupils have heard it many times at home, and probably in the classroom, too. They have been saying it ever since the terrible two's. They have the oral–aural background necessary to learn to read and write the word *no*.

Print *no* on an index card, and present it, saying, "This is the word *no*." If your pupil knows the sound /n/, call attention to it at the beginning of the word *no*. Also, say the name of the letter o (the long sound /ō/), and demonstrate how you can blend the sounds into the word *no*.

Be prepared for a few early learners to display reversal tendencies (or just plain confusion) and get mixed up between the word *no* and the word *on*. The juxtaposition of the letters of *no* and *on* is common in early writing. The miscue in word recognition is common in early reading. Sometimes it helps to show children *No* with a capital N to emphasize the sound /n/ at the beginning.

To lead into a "yes or no" game, tell your pupil:

> *When you learn to read the words yes and no,*
> *we can play question-and-answer games.*
> *Lots of questions have yes or no answers.*
> *You can hold up a wordcard to answer me,*
> *and I can hold up a wordcard to answer you.*

Have your child trace the word *no* with a finger, write it in sand, put it together with felt or magnetic letters, trace it on paper, write it with a crayon, or print it on the chalkboard, depending on the child's abilities as a writer.

After the child recognizes the word *no*, use similar procedures to present the word *yes* from a wordcard. Point out that it looks different from the word *no*, and that it also sounds different. Use writing and phonics to reinforce the reading of the word.

Take a vote on some classroom issue by having each child write *yes* or *no* on a ballot.

When the child can distinguish between *yes* and *no*, start the question game. Ask questions that can be answered by holding up the *yes* card or the *no* card. At first your questions should be very easy so that the child can focus on reading the cards and holding up the right one.

Is your name Rumplestiltskin?
Do you have hair on your head?
Do you wear pajamas at school?
Do you hear stories at school?
Did you eat breakfast this morning?
Do you like to go to bed early?

When your children's ability to read the words *yes* and *no* seems firm, your questions can relate to other things you are teaching in your early 3 Rs program.

Is today Wednesday?
Can you count to five?
Is this month February?
Have you printed your name today?
Can you write the number five?
Did you hear your favorite story at read-aloud time?

Some of these yes-or-no questions will promote discussion, and that's fine. Your pupil is showing comprehension of sight words, reviewing learnings in other areas, and perhaps thinking beyond yes-and-no answers.

Getting Active With "Down" and "Up"

Print the words *down* and *up* on index cards. Show only the *down* card to your early reader. Point out the letter d and the sound /d/ at the beginning of the word *down*, and the letter n and the sound /n/ at the end, if the child is familiar with these sounds.

Ask the child, "What do you see when you look down?" Press for a lot of answers—shoes, socks, jeans, legs of a chair, the floor, anything that is on the floor.

After a few days, when your child recognizes *down*, you can use similar procedures to teach the word *up*. Discuss the meaning of *up*. Ask, "What do you see when you look up?" If you are standing when you ask the question, "you" should be one of the child's answers.

For active review, play with the words *up* and *down* on a flight of stairs. Have your pupil take one step up or one step down, depending on what card you show. You can also use the cards to instruct your pupil to toss a ball or a beanbag up through a basket, or down into a bag.

For pupils who can recognize the verbs *jumps* and *climbs*, you can bring together art, reading, and writing. Fold a large paper in half. On one side print "Spot jumps down." On the other side, print "Spot jumps up." Have Spot's owner draw a picture to match each sentence.

Suppose a pupil named Kathleen was good at climbing trees and at writing. She could write "Kathleen climbs up" and "Kathleen climbs down," and illustrate her own sentences.

CONCEPT BOOKS ON OPPOSITES

Although you are teaching *no* and *yes*, *down* and *up*, you are no doubt still reading aloud to your pupils. Concept books on opposites would be good choices for read-aloud time, because some of them feature these pairs of words. Perhaps you can find one or more of these titles, or other books about opposites, in your library.

- Banchek, L. *Snake in, snake out.* Crowell.
- Burningham, J. *Opposites.* Crown.
- Hill, E. *Opposites peek-a-boo.* Price/Stern/Sloan.
- Hoban, T. *Big ones, little ones.* Greenwillow.
- Hoban, T. *Exactly the opposite.* Greenwillow.
- Leedy, L. *Big small, short, tall.* Holiday House.
- Spier, P. *Fast-slow, high-low: A book of opposites.* Doubleday.

NOTING DEGREES OF SUCCESS

You can expect wide variation in your degrees of success with helping beginners recognize *no*, *yes*, *down*, and *up*. Not all of your early learners will hold onto their recognition of these words. The children who can distinguish among the four words today may appear to have forgotten them tomorrow. Some pupils who can read the words from wordcards will not recognize them in print in a book. Only your most capable early learners will read and write *no*, *yes*, *down*, and *up* as quickly and easily as they handled nouns and verbs.

If a pupil has considerable difficulty with these words, remember that you were just "testing the waters" to see if the time was right for moving beyond concrete nouns and action verbs. Maybe it's not. The child can go forward in other areas, so there is no need to push this particular area.

If, however, you find that a good number of your pupils learn *no*, *yes*, *down*, and *up* with relative ease, then you might want to consider working on these words with the whole class. One by one, gradually, these words may get posted on your word wall.

23

◆ ◆ ◆

Teach the Whole Alphabet for Reading, Writing, and Phonics

Overview

These are the topics you will meet in this chapter:

- Alphabet Books for Letter Names and Sounds
- Sorting and Matching Capital and Lower-Case Letters
- Final Sounds in Words
- Partner Blending of Onset and Rhyme
- Letter-Sound Relationships in Most Phonics Programs

ALPHABET BOOKS FOR LETTER NAMES AND SOUNDS

Your pupils who took the first steps into phonics can probably tell you the sounds of a number of consonant letters. Your Betty's and your Bert's recognize their initial B and can tell you, "The letter B stands for the sound /b/." They have probably mastered eight or ten other initial letter-sound correspondences from words they came to know by sight on wordcards.

However, they may not know a sound for every letter of the alphabet. They may not yet have extended their phonemic awareness to final sounds in words. They may not have mastered blending. So you can select from among a number of approaches for your next steps in the early teaching of phonics.

Many commercial phonics programs take young children through the whole alphabet in a highly structured fashion. They are effective with some pupils, but others do better with the more informal approach of alphabet books for initial letter-sound relationships.

At read-aloud time, you can give special attention to the letters of the alphabet that each of your early learners may need. Any alphabet book will do, but here are some especially good ones:

- Anno, M. *Anno's alphabet.* Crowell.
- Demi. *Find the animals ABC.* Grosset and Dunlap.
- Feelings, M. *Jambo means hello: Swahili alphabet book.* Dial.
- Gag, W. *The ABC bunny.* Coward McCann.
- Lobel, A. *On market street.* Scholastic.
- MacDonald, S. *Alphabatics.* Bradbury Press.
- VanAllsburg, C. *The Z was zapped.* Houghton Mifflin.
- Viorst, J. *The alphabet from Z to A.* Atheneum.
- Wildsmith, B. *Brian Wildsmith's ABC.* Watts.

Suppose you were teaching a pupil named Michael, and he had no word that started with the letter H in his wordbank of cards. You would want Michael to help you read the H/h page of the alphabet book. As he identified the pictures of the hat, horn, head, and ham on the H page, you would repeat his words, emphasizing the breathy sound /h/ at the beginning of each word. Then you would point to the capital H and the lower-case h on the page, and tell him directly, "The letter H stands for the sound /h/."

You would use similar procedures with another early reader who had no wordcards that started with the letter V. With this individualized approach, you still personalize your early teaching of initial–consonant phonics while working with a group at read-aloud time.

Most elementary alphabet books give you letters, words, and pictures, but expect you to make up your own questions about each page. Lara Holtz's *Alphabet Book* (Dorling Kindersley Ltd.), however, includes text and questions. On the B page, for example, there are pictures of nineteen babies in action. You can read: "Search for a baby brushing his teeth. Spot a bear bib. Say 'Boo' to the baby under the basket … How many babies are building with blocks. Find a baby blowing bubbles." This and other more advanced alphabet books promote counting and vocabulary development along with letter recognition and phonics.

Sorting and Matching Capital and Lower-Case Letters

Alphabet books usually show both the big A and the little a on the page with pictures of apples. These books are helpful not only with the matching of letters with sounds but also with the matching of the capital with the lower-case form of each letter.

Have your alphabet-learners do matching activities. Make or buy some decks of alphabet cards, at least two decks of capital letters and two decks of lower-case letters. When you want a child to practice matching capital letters, lay out one deck of capitals on the table, face up, in sequential order. From the other deck of capitals, have the child draw a card. Suppose the child draws the letter N. Then say, "Cover the N on the table."

Use the same procedure with lower-case letters, and then for matching the capital and lower-case forms of each letter.

FINAL SOUNDS IN WORDS

Beginners seem to be able to focus on the initial sound in a word much more easily than the final sound. In fact, final sounds are often neglected or ignored, even by first and second graders. Therefore, it is important in your early phonics program to build phonemic awareness of final sounds in words.

When you want your children to listen for same and different sounds at the ends of words, you can tell them:

> *I'm going to say two names.*
> *Do they end with the same sound*
> *or with different sounds? Pat, Pam.*

If you emphasize the final sound of each word, some of your children may be able to figure out that *Pat* and *Pam* end with different sounds. Other pairs of first names that end with different sounds are *Al* and *Ann*, *Ben* and *Beth*, *Kim* and *Kip*, and *Joan* and *Joel*.

Pairs of first names that end in the same sound include *Jed* and *Todd*, *Dan* and *Lynn*, and *Dick* and *Mac*. If you move to last names, you can come up with a group that end in the sound /z/, such as *Martinez*, *Ramirez*, *Cortez*, and *Diaz*.

When you add context clues to your oral activities on final sounds, you might try these name game possibilities with a child:

> — *There's a girl in our class whose name ends*
> *with the sound /n/. Who is she?* (Kyleen)
> — *There is a boy in our class whose name*
> *ends with the sound /l/. Who is he?* (Jamail)
> — *I'm thinking of a gray animal at the zoo. The*
> *name of this animal ends in the sound /t/.*
> *What animal is it?* (elephant)
> — *I spy something that has an author. Its name*
> *ends in the sound /k/. What is it?* (book)

To connect letters in print to final sounds, you might start with a wordcard for the word *run*. You could say:

> *Look at the word <u>run</u> in print.*
> *It has three letters—r u n.*
> *The last letter in <u>run</u> is n.*
> *The word <u>run</u> ends with the sound /n/.*
> *Let's say that sound together—/n/*

Then say "Runnnnnnnn," stretching out the /n/ final sound in the word to emphasize it.

The blending of sounds into words is the payoff of phonics. To demonstrate blending, you could again hold up the wordcard for *run* and say:

> *Usually you remember the word <u>run</u> as soon as*
> *you look at it. But if you ever forget the word,*
> *you can use phonics to help you sound it out.*
> *The first letter r stands for the sound /r/.*
> *The last letter n stands for the sound /n/.*
> *When you blend the sounds of the three*
> *letters, r - u - n, you get the word <u>run</u>.*

Have your pupil listen as you blend the sounds in the word *run*, slowly at first, then faster. Point to each letter as you make each sound. Slide your finger from the r to the u to the n as you draw out the sounds. Ask your pupil to extend the sound /n/ as long as you keep your finger on the letter n, the final sound.

Although very few of your pupils may have learned that the letter u stands for the sound "uh," they can still understand what you are doing when you demonstrate blending.

Partner Blending of Onset and Rhyme

In another approach to blending, you and your pupil work as partners. You make the sound of an initial consonant in a word (the onset sound), and your pupil supplies the sound of the word-family ending (the rhyme). For example, you say /s/ and your pupil says *at*, to arrive at the word *sat*. Then you say /f/ and your pupil says *at*, to arrive at the word *fat*.

Many short, simple words are in such rhyming word families as *et* (bet, met, pet, wet), *ip* (dip, chip, lip, tip), *ock* (block, clock, lock, knock), and *un* (bun, fun, run, sun).

You and your pupils could agree to start with the *an* family (can, Dan, fan, man, pan, ran, tan, van). As soon as you say the sound /c/, your pupil says *an*. Then you ask, "What's that word?"

If the child is able to put the sounds together to make the word *can*, great! If not, demonstrate by running together the sounds faster and faster until you blend them into the word *can*.

You and your pupil might be able to use the same partnering strategy to produce *fan, pan, man,* and all the other words in the *an* family.

Partner blending helps the beginner during the "catching on" period. This period may be lengthy, because blending is a skill that some young children are slow to master orally, and even slower to apply to print. The teaching of blending continues through the primary grades.

LETTER-SOUND RELATIONSHIPS
IN MOST PHONICS PROGRAMS

Phonics programs may differ about what sounds to teach first, how many different sounds each letter can stand for, or what sound or spelling relationships to present. They usually agree, however, about the most frequently used sounds of letters. So you are making a sure-to-be-useful contribution to your child's education when you teach the basic letter-sound relationships.

At the beginning of a word or syllable, these consonant letters usually stand for the initial sounds in the key words:

Letter	*Key Word*
B	bee
D	day
F	fall
H	hi
J	jay
K	key
L	low
M	me
N	no
P	pie
Q	quit
R	row
S	say
T	tea
V	van
W	way
Z	zip

Most phonics programs point out that the consonant c can stand for the hard sound /k/ as in *cane* or the soft sound /s/ as in *cider*. They also agree that the consonant g can stand for the hard sound /g/ as in *gum* or the soft sound /j/ as in *giraffe*. Some programs refer to the "hard" and "soft" sounds as the "first" and "second" sounds, respectively.

Sooner or later, all phonics programs include the long and short sounds of the vowels. The long sound of each vowel is its name. Key words are helpful for remembering the short sounds.

Vowel	Key Word for Short Sound	Key Word for Long Sound
A	at	ate
E	end	eve
I	in	ice
O	otter	old
U	us	use

Each key word features a vowel in the initial position, but vowels occur most often in medial positions. So you may need to help some of your early readers hear and see the differences in groups of words such as:

cat	cot	cut
bag	beg	big
lad	led	lid
sang	sing	song
tack	tick	tuck

Much of the teaching of medial vowel sounds, however, continues into the primary grades. If you help an early learner begin to use vowel phonics to sound out words, both you and the child are far ahead of the game.

The letter y appears most frequently at the ends of words, where it stands for the long e sound, as in *Mommy, Daddy, baby*, and *funny*. The second most frequent sound of the letter y is the long i sound, as in *my, by*, and *fly*. The least frequent sound of y is the consonant sound at the beginning of such words as *yard, yellow*, and *year*.

The letter x can stand for the sound of ks as in *fox*, and the sound of z as in *xylophone*.

Many other sounds of vowels and consonants are presented in formal, structured phonics programs. They often include consonant blends formed with l (bl, cl, fl, gl, pl, sl), r (br, cr, dr, gr, pr, tr), and s (sc, sk, sl, sm, sn, sp, st, sw). Beginners may learn to blend three consonants at the beginning of such words as *scratch*, *spring*, and *street*.

Phonics programs also introduce consonant digraphs as two letters that form a new sound, such as ch in *church*, sh as in *she*, ph as in *phone*, ng as in *ring*, and th as in *then* (voiced) or *thin* (voiceless).

Diphthongs (sliding vowel sounds) are presented in most phonics programs, but not until after the children have learned basic consonant and vowel sounds. Usually the first four diphthongs to be featured are oy as in *boy*, oi as in *oil*, ow as in *cow*, and ou as in *out*.

For your early 3 Rs program, however, you want to stay with the basics. Your readers and writers will have a good phonics foundation for the primary grades if they have developed phonemic awareness, alphabet recognition, and association of the letters with their most common sounds.

24

◆ ◆ ◆

Stimulate New Areas
of Language Development

<table>
<tr><td>

Overview

These are the topics you will meet in this chapter:

- The Hearing, Saying, Reading, and Writing Progression
- Building Vocabulary With Specific Words
- Developing Fluency in Oral and Written Language
- Using Wordless Books for Composing
- Author-Illustrators of Wordless Books

</td></tr>
</table>

THE HEARING, SAYING, READING, AND WRITING PROGRESSION

Immersion in the oral language of the 3 Rs was the first preparatory activity you used with your early learners of reading, writing, and arithmetic. You also promoted their language development through activities with oral and written language in your print-rich room.

By now, some of your early learners can progress into new areas of vocabulary growth and language development. As always, they must start with oral words and sentences, and then progress to the printed forms.

You know that beginners are comfortable reading only those words with which they have already built familiarity from oral use. You would definitely build a child's oral familiarity with the word *aquarium*, for example, before you would even consider presenting it in print. The child should talk about, see, touch, and even smell an aquarium before working with the word in print.

The building of oral familiarity and comfort is essential not only for vocabulary growth but also for language development in terms of sentence reading. Young children cannot comfortably read sentences that are longer and more complex than the sentences they use in speech. So, in your conversations and lessons with your pupils, you want to discourage their answering in monosyllables and encourage their speaking in full sentences.

Let's consider some "how to do it" approaches that promote vocabulary growth beyond the essential 3 Rs vocabulary and enhance language development. You can start by encouraging your children to use specific words rather than general terms, and to speak in complete and well-developed sentences. You can continue by using wordless books to build fluency in written language.

BUILDING VOCABULARY
WITH SPECIFIC WORDS

Many early learners are dinosaur enthusiasts. They take delight in books about dinosaurs. At read-aloud time, you can keep them fascinated by talking about the pictures of dinosaurs in books for older children, informational books, even museum books. If you use the names, brontosaurus, ankylosaurus, and tyrannosaurus rex, you'll soon hear your dinosaur enthusiasts picking up those words.

If a pupil sees an insect and calls it a "bug," you should answer, "Yes, that is a cricket (or an ant or beetle)." In this way, you are building the child's vocabulary by giving him or her the specific word for the insect, rather than passively accepting the general term *bug*. You can encourage the child to use the specific word in talking further about the insect. Suppose you ask, "How would you describe the cricket to a friend who was blindfolded?" Your pupil would almost have to use the word *cricket* repeatedly in the description.

Suppose you ask a child the question, "What did you have for lunch?" Don't settle for just "A sandwich" as the answer. You want to lead the child to tell you specifically what kind of sandwich. Tuna and bologna might be new words to the peanut butter devotee. Even if the child says, "A cheese sandwich," you can inquire further. "Swiss cheese? American cheese? Mozzarella cheese?"

At snack time you can talk to a child about the *platter* of crackers because the child may not know the word for this familiar object. Many young children are not clear on the differences between a plate, a saucer, and a bowl, so they need to hear you using the terms in context.

You can use the word game Categories to increase children's vocabularies of specific words that belong to general categories. The first player names a category, furniture, for example. Each succeeding player has to name a different piece of furniture. The first person who misses must start a new category. In the case of furniture, such specific words as *chair*, *table*, and *bed* usually come forth quickly. Then, if there is a pause, it is time for you to encourage your players to use illustrations in picture books to help them think of more pieces of furniture.

If you yourself regularly use specific words rather than general terms, you are helping your children expand their vocabularies.

DEVELOPING FLUENCY IN ORAL
AND WRITTEN LANGUAGE

Some pupils speak in very short sentences and answer questions in monosyllables. You want to help these children develop fluency and achieve a greater command of oral language. Your pupils will pattern their sentences on the ones they hear from you, so it is important that you provide opportunities for them to imitate you.

You can do this by asking them to relay information around the class.

Suppose you told a quiet child that you wanted her to pass along to her classmates everything you told her about the items in the Lost and Found. Then you said, "There are two sweaters, a red one and a blue one. The red one is a pullover, and the blue one has buttons." You might then get the child to rehearse with you, and give the information back to you in well-developed sentences, before passing it on to another pupil.

Sentence expansion games are another approach for helping children formulate longer sentences. To start, you could say, "There's a chalkboard in our classroom."

Your pupil has to add something to what you've said, so the child might add the color of the chalkboard, saying, "There's a green chalkboard in our classroom."

Then you could expand the sentence a bit more by saying, "There's a green chalkboard with a scratch on it in our classroom."

The child may have to think for a moment before adding, "There's a green chalkboard with a scratch on it in our classroom, but I didn't make the scratch."

At that point you might want to start a new sentence.

Another way that you can encourage your pupils to speak fluently is to ask questions that require more than one-word answers.

- *What would you do if a storm knocked out all the electricity at your home and you had no lights?*
- *What do you think would happen if a lost kitten followed you home?*
- *If someone asked you "What did you learn in school today," what would you say?*

USING WORDLESS BOOKS FOR COMPOSING

Wordless books (also called *textless books*) are good tools for developing fluency of language. These excellently illustrated books depend on the pictures to tell the story. Because there is absolutely no text on the pages, the illustrations have to communicate the sequence of events.

When you and your pupils examine the illustrations together, allow plenty of time for talking. Your children may disagree about the direction of the story. You may need to help them follow the sequence of events from the illustrations. Eventually they can orally compose a story that goes with the pictures. Of course, they'll need to come up with complete, well-developed sentences for their story.

Sometimes one of your early writers will actually try to print a sentence that the group composes. But most of your pupils will want you to do the writing as they compose, because that is much faster. Once they dictate a sentence or two for each page, the book is no longer wordless. Its story is told in your pupils' own words. And it is told fluently.

The next day, after you read your pupils' story back to them, encourage them to try to read it. Their readings probably won't be word-for-word renditions of the sentences you printed. Some parts of their story may sound more "memorized" than read as they repeat certain sentences. Other parts may be embellished with new ideas. But consider all the good things that are happening in terms of language development.

Your pupils looked at a book without words, and they gave it words. *Their* words! They composed a story, using their own vocabulary. They told the story in well-developed sentences. You (or they) wrote the story for subsequent rereading. This rereading demonstrated the writing–reading connection.

Wordless books enable you to do with a group, or with your whole class, what you did with the individual child who dictated her retelling of a folktale to the tape recorder (chap. 19). With the individual child, you proceeded (top-down) to transcribe her story from the tape-recorded version and show it to her in print. You then read it aloud to her. Thereafter, you and she read parts of the story together, and proceeded to focus on a particular sentence that you cut apart into words that she could learn to recognize.

The story your pupils compose for a wordless book will contain words that some children will learn to recognize and will want for their wordbanks. So wordless books can help your early learners increase not only their oral language fluency but also their reading and writing vocabularies.

Author–Illustrators of Wordless Books

Some popular illustrators have created whole series of books without words. You can find a good selection of wordless books in most libraries. Any of these titles (or whatever other wordless books are available to you) will serve the instructional purposes of your early 3 Rs program:

- Alexander, M. *Out, out, out*. Dial.
- Carle, E. *Do you want to be my friend?* Crowell.
- DePaola, T. *Pancakes for breakfast*. Harcourt Brace.
- Goodall, J. S. *Story of the seashore*. Macmillan.
- Keats, E. *Kitten for a day*. Watts.
- Mayer, M. *A boy, a dog, and a frog*. Dial.
- McCully, E. A. *New baby*. Harper.
- Spier, P. *Noah's ark*. Doubleday.
- Weisner, D. *Tuesday*. Farrar.

Each rereading of a story composed from a wordless book is another opportunity for language activities. You can copy sentences from the story on strips of paper to clip to the book. Then it is no longer wordless. For some of your pupils, it may even be relatively easy-to-read. Children can usually read a story written in their own words more easily than a story written by someone else. So they may return to the "book without words" on their own and read it.

By encouraging your children to use specific words and to speak and write in well-developed sentences, you are promoting their vocabulary growth and language development.

25

$$\blacklozenge \quad \blacklozenge \quad \blacklozenge$$

Summary of Unit III

HOW TO EXPAND AND VARY STRATEGIES FOR EARLY TEACHING OF THE 3 Rs

The chapters in Unit III present teaching strategies that you can use to expand your early 3 Rs instructional program. To help your pupils progress beyond the first steps in reading, writing, or arithmetic, you can vary your methods and materials in the following ways.

Use Software and Equipment to Enrich Your Teaching

When your pupils make audiotapes of their retellings of stories, you can write sentence from these tapes. Often your pupils can learn to read their own spoken words in these sentences. You might also enrich classic stories by showing videotapes. Computer literacy has to start early, because you want to use CD-ROMs in your early 3 Rs program. Simple measurement equipment will help some of your children make further progress in early arithmetic.

Move Toward Math Operations With Children's Books

At read-aloud time you can present and discuss stories that help to develop your pupils' concepts of addition, subtraction, multiplication, and division. Children's books can also help with the teaching of sorting, measuring, and telling time.

Start a Word Wall of Pupils' Names in Alphabetical Order

As a group activity, your whole class can build a word wall of words for reading and writing. The first group of words to be posted are the first names of all the pupils in the class. Each child, in alphabetical order, has an individual word wall day for the posting of his or her name.

Go Beyond Concrete Nouns and Action Verbs

Your early learners probably have good collections of wordcards of nouns and action verbs, learned mainly through the first-steps strategies. By using new strategies, you can help some of your pupils learn different types of words, such as *no* and *yes*, and *down* and *up*.

Teach the Whole Alphabet for Reading, Writing, and Phonics

To help your child progress in phonics, you can introduce him or her to hearing, isolating, and identifying the sound of each letter of the alphabet. Early learners can benefit from activities with alphabet books, phonemic awareness games that focus on the final sounds in words, and blending practice.

Stimulate New Areas of Language Development

Your use of specific words rather than general terms can promote vocabulary growth for your early learners. Relaying information and expanding sentences can promote their language development. Your pupils can also benefit from composing stories for books without words.

Unit IV

◆ ◆ ◆

How to Smooth the Transition Into 3 Rs in the Primary Grades

26

◆ ◆ ◆

Preview of Unit IV:
Move Smoothly Into
the Primary Grades

Throughout your early 3 Rs program, you have been preparing your pupils to succeed with reading, writing, and arithmetic in the primary grades. Now what final steps can you take—especially with those children who have moved most rapidly and successfully through your program?

In the primary grades, children continue to learn from many of the informal approaches you have already introduced in your early 3 Rs program. Yet activities for the primary grades are increasingly structured. Your transitional steps, therefore, will move toward more structured approaches for promoting further growth in reading, writing, and arithmetic.

WHAT TO DO

Your early learners who can progress through the following activities will make smooth transitions into 3 Rs in the primary grades. To help them, you can:

- Strengthen *when* and *where* concepts as background for print.
- Teach games that require early arithmetic.
- Lead pupils to model on pattern books, using phonics for writing and reading.
- Present high-frequency words in developmentally appropriate ways.
- Use the library to extend their reading, writing, and arithmetic.

Some teachers devote time to all of these activities on the same day, since there is no preferred order. Others introduce only one or two to selected pupils. Whatever way you schedule these activities, they can bring about still more development in the 3 Rs for those pupils who have done well as early learners of reading, writing, and arithmetic.

WHY TO DO IT

Transitional activities introduce more structure into the early learning of the 3 Rs. They help young children move from the personalized approaches of the early first steps to the structured approaches of the primary grades.

How can you smooth the transition in reading? By presenting some high-frequency words. Nouns and verbs are fine for the first steps in reading. But your early learners now need to recognize some high-frequency words if they are to progress beyond simple noun-and-verb sentence structures. Prepositions, conjunctions, pronouns, and determiners are numerous even in easy-to-read library books, so you want to start introducing such words in developmentally appropriate ways.

How can you smooth the transition in writing? By helping your pupils model on pattern stories. Their own personalized stories are fine for the first steps in writing, but such stories have very little structure. You can help your pupils add structure to their writing by teaching them to identify and imitate predictable patterns in children's books.

How can you smooth the transition in arithmetic? By teaching your children some math games. Their counting books are fine for the first steps in arithmetic. But they now need practice in applying mathematical thinking in the structured situation of a game.

Even as you move into transitional activities with some of your pupils, you want to maintain the activities described in Units I, II, and III. You can continue to foster growth for all your children through such Unit I approaches as arithme-talk, environmental print, and daily read-aloud sessions with participation extras. Most of the first-steps activities in Unit II involved individualized teaching, and you certainly have some pupils who learn best with one-to-one instruction. So, for them, you'll continue with personalized wordbanks, storybooks, and counting books.

Many of the strategies in Unit III were beneficial for small groups or for your whole class, so they should be continued. A few Unit III activities can be viewed as somewhat transitional in that teachers in the primary grades may use word walls, edu-taining CD-ROMs, and wordless books. So perhaps you have already started smoothing the transition as you broadened and varied the strategies in your early 3 Rs program.

You want to seize the teachable moment for each stage of progress, and some of your early learners are probably showing you signs that they can handle more structure. However, some children who learned easily from the early first-steps strategies will not be able to handle all these structured transitional activities. This is no cause for concern, of course, because these activities extend well into the primary grades.

Use your discretion about how far to try to take each of your early learners. Remember that the *final* steps in the early 3 Rs are really only the beginning steps in the child's education.

27

◆ ◆ ◆

Strengthen <u>When</u> and <u>Where</u> Concepts as Background for Print

Overview

These are the topics you will meet in this chapter:

- Numbers and Words That Answer the Question, "When?"
- Arithme-Talk About Birthdays
- Words That Answer the Question, "Where?"
- Reinforcing Position Concepts
- From Speech to Print for a Position Word
- Working Toward the Word Wall

NUMBERS AND WORDS THAT ANSWER THE QUESTION, "WHEN?"

You used arithme-talk to develop number concepts before you helped your early learners make counting books. You wanted to be sure that each child understood the concepts of "one," "two," "three," and "four" before the child tried to associate those concepts with the symbols 1, 2, 3, and 4 in print in a counting book or on the calendar.

In the same way, you want to be sure that an early learner has internalized the concepts associated with the frequently used words that answer the questions "When?" and "Where?" Then you can gradually present such words for reading and writing.

Every day of the school year, you call your pupils' attention to words that answer the question "When?" On your classroom calendar you point at and read not only a number for the date, but also words for the day of the week and the month of the year. When you say, "Today is Thursday, March 9," you are answering the question "When?" with words and numbers. All year you've been building your children's concepts of dates, days, months, and probably seasons and holidays.

As a result of the concept-building, daily repetition, and initial consonant phonics, some of your early learners may already be able to identify the words *Monday, Wednesday,* and *Friday.* They may need additional clues to differentiate *Tuesday* from *Thursday* (because both start with capital T) and *Saturday* from *Sunday* (because your pupils are not with you on weekends).

As with all environmental print, however, the words "take" with some pupils and not with others. But for those students who have been giving active attention to your calendar talk, wordcards for weekdays are easy additions to their wordbanks.

Some children want wordcards for the month of their birthday and for holidays. If the interest is there, these words are relatively easy for early readers and writers to learn. Sometimes you get a bonus for all your good teaching: You discover that a child can recognize some words you never formally presented.

As you add groups of words to your word wall, consider the days of the week, the months of the year, and even the words for numbers. Maybe your whole class can learn to recognize them.

The numbers on the calendar certainly help with your teaching of number concepts. But some of your pupils do not really internalize concepts beyond the single-digit numbers. There is one number, however, that commands special attention—the date of a child's birthday.

Arithme-Talk About Birthdays

Suppose that Joe's birthday is on May 19. On May 1, you and he can start counting the days until his birthday on the calendar. On May 2, he can count again, and see that it is one day less. On May 3 and 4, his counting shows his birthday is getting closer and closer.

No countdown for a rocket launch is more important than the countdown toward a birthday for a young child. This calendar activity can be an exciting extension of arithme-talk for the birthday children each month.

Sequence-of-events pictures have special significance at birthday time. Pictures of (1) wrapping presents, (2) opening presents, and (3) cleaning up can correspond with discussions of what happens *before, during,* and *after* the birthday party. Arithme-talk about the concepts of before, during, and after should, of course, precede showing the words in print. But if you print *before, during,* and *after,* along with 1, 2, and 3 on the backs of the sequence-of-events pictures, some of your early learners may start connecting the words with the concepts.

WORDS THAT ANSWER
THE QUESTION, "WHERE?"

Some of the shortest, simplest prepositions in our language embody concepts that answer the important question "Where?" Concepts of position or location are expressed by such frequently used words as *in, above, below, on, behind,* and *under.* Your pupils need to understand these location concepts, and to use the words for them with ease orally, before they encounter the words in print.

In playing hide and seek, they have positioned themselves *behind* the door, *in* the hall, or *under* the table, so most of them comprehend these prepositions to some degree. But you may want to strengthen the degree before you lead your early learners to read and write position words that answer the question "Where?"

Reinforcing Position Concepts

Tana Hoban created the textless book, *All about where* (Greenwillow), in which the photos show "above, on, behind, under, out, against, across, between, in, through, beside, among, below, over, around."

One photo shows people *between* lamp posts, walking *across* a bridge *over* a river. A boat is going *around* its route *through* an arch *under* the bridge. *Among* the passengers are some who are *out on* deck, some who are *below* a canopy, and some who are leaning *against* the rails, *beside* one another. *In* the background are buildings *behind* trees with a blue sky *above.*

This photo offers many opportunities for "where" questions. Of course, you want speaking, not pointing, from your pupils as they reply to your questions about locations and positions.

When you hold up the boat photo for your class and ask, "Where are the passengers?" you'd like your pupils to answer in complete sentences. But if it seems artificial to insist on a full sentence for every answer, you can at least require location phrases. "In the boat." "Out on deck." "Leaning against the rails." "Standing beside one another." You can promote this type of concept reinforcement and language development with almost any picture or photo, if you ask questions about positions and locations.

Another way to strengthen position concepts is with a shelf activity. If your room has shelves, you are all set with top, middle, and bottom levels. If there are no shelves in your room, you can use a table, a chair seat, and the floor, as the top, middle, and bottom levels. Place a box on the middle shelf (or middle level). The box should be open, and facing you. Your pupil should have six cards. Give these directions orally to your pupil:

Put a card in the box.
Put a card above the box.
Put a card below the box.
Put a card on the box.
Put a card behind the box.
Put a card under the box.

Most children will interpret *below* in terms of the bottom shelf and *above* in terms of the top shelf. But occasionally a child will lift the box to slip a card under it when you say, "Put a card below the box."

If this happens, say, "Suppose you couldn't lift the box. Suppose there was not the tiniest bit of room beneath the box to slide in a card. Then how would you put a card below the box?" This question will probably get the child to put the card on the bottom shelf. Of course, lifting the box is the correct response for "Put a card under the box." Use the same type of questioning if a child interprets *above* as *on top of*.

From Speech to Print for a Position Word

When your pupil is sure of the position concepts, make wordcards for *in*, *above*, *below*, *on*, *behind*, and *under*. The word *in* is probably the easiest to read because it is short and phonetically regular. It is a blend of the sounds /i/ and /n/, so it yields to phonics. Also, the child has been hearing and using the word *in* for years, so the oral–aural background is strong. To present *in*, you might say:

Let's read this word together—in.
We can sound it out—/i/ /n/, and
blend the sounds together—in.

To get extra mileage out of the box activity, you could add, "When I hand you the *in* wordcard, put it in the box."

But don't expect your early learners to remember the word *in* after the first exposure. Each child will need to review the *in* wordcard frequently. Only a few will be quick to read and write the word. Even fewer will reach the point of being able to approach the box and correctly read and place each of the wordcards bearing the words *in*, *above*, *below*, *on*, *behind*, and *under*.

WORKING TOWARD THE WORD WALL

Words that answer the questions "When?" and "Where?" are used very frequently in our language, both in speech and in print. Therefore, you want to promote their comprehension and their use by your students in your early 3 Rs program.

Your pupils need to be able to read and write these words in order to move along toward literacy. Even if not every pupil in your class can identify and recall these words, they are worth whole-group attention and discussion. Keep working toward posting them on your word wall.

28

◆ ◆ ◆

Play Games That Require
Early Arithmetic

Overview

These are the topics you will meet in this chapter:

- Contests and Games for a Gentle Transition
- Spinners and Dice
- Jumping Contests
- More or Less
- Guess-timating
- Concentration
- Hide and Find
- Independent Extensions

CONTESTS AND GAMES
FOR A GENTLE TRANSITION

By now, some of your early learners are counting quite comfortably. For these children, you may want to treat the transition into early arithmetic as an extension of counting. Math-oriented games and contests provide opportunities to help your pupils play their way through the transition.

Spinners and Dice

You can make, buy, or acquire from the parents of your pupils some board games that use spinners and dice to indicate the number of spaces a player can move. These games provide both playful and practical applications of counting.

A player who uses two dice is approaching addition, although many beginners just count all the dots on the two top faces. Of course, that type of counting helps a child grasp the concept of addition.

Jumping Contests

Right in front of your measuring center (or outdoors), your pupils can have jumping contests. How far can each player jump? Your early learners will pull out the tape measure of inches and feet as they compete.

Jumping games promote more addition (and writing of numbers for record-keeping) when they are played in small teams. Each team member gets two jumps. The sum of the measurements of the two jumps is that player's score. The team with the highest score wins.

More or Less

This card game is popular with early learners who can count to 10, can read the numbers 2 to 10, and can comprehend the order of progression of those numbers.

From a regular deck of playing cards, use only the ones that show the numbers from 2 to 10. Pile those cards in a stack.

Draw a card from the stack. Let's say you drew a 5. Tell your pupil, "Try to guess the number I drew."

Suppose the child guesses, "3."

Then you say, "No, my number is higher. It's more than 3."

Suppose the child then guesses, "6."

You reply, "No, my number is lower. It's less than 6."

Proceed in this pattern until the child figures out the number. You may want to keep a number ladder nearby to help your beginner.

When it becomes your turn to guess the number that the child drew, you may want to demonstrate how to use the ladder's sequence of numbers to help with the guessing.

Guess-timating

Suppose you hold up a plastic cup of grapes and invite each child in your class to guess how many grapes are in the cup. The child who comes closest is the winner of the guess-timating game.

Of course, young children are usually more interested in the activity itself than in winning. So the fascinating thing about the guess-timating game is watching how some of your early learners approach estimating.

One may guess 100 simply because he or she knows it's a large number. Another may try to count all the grapes that are visible. You can help the children who are good at the "More or Less" game by asking them:

Do you think it's less than 100 grapes?
Do you think it's more than 10 grapes?

For variety, the guess-timating game can involve other objects such as apples in a bag, paperclips in a necklace, or rocks in a pail. The things you choose should be developmentally appropriate for the skills of your class. Seeds are too tiny; anything smaller than pennies is probably not useful.

Concentration

This game is a classic that can be adapted for any level of ability, because you choose how many cards (and what cards) you will use from a deck of regular playing cards.

The object of the game is to remember where the matching cards are placed so that you can match and collect pairs. You probably want to use at least eight cards with your pupil (two rows of four cards each), so you would prepare for the game by selecting from the deck four pairs of cards with matching numbers.

Place the cards face down on the table in front of your pupil. Say, "Turn two cards face-up so that you can see the numbers on them. Do they match?"

If the answer is yes, the child gets to keep the two cards. If the answer is no, the cards must be tuned over again, face down.

Now, however, the players know the locations of two numbers. Suppose, on the next turn, a player turns up a number that has been shown before. Then the player will use his or her memory to make a pair by choosing to turn up a card in a specific location.

Hide and Find

You can prepare your early counters for subtraction when you play "Hide and Find" with them. To start the game, you would hide four balls and tell your pupil to find them. After each find, you would ask,

How many of the balls have you found?
How many more do you have to look for?

The child would have to answer your questions in terms of these situations: (a) 1 ball found and 3 to look for, (b) 2 balls found and 2 to look for, (c) 3 balls found and 1 to look for, and (d) all 4 balls found.

INDEPENDENT EXTENSIONS

After you have taught any of these basic games to some of your early learners, your pupils can play with each other, independent of you. They may opt for high numbers to add greater complexity to these transitional math games.

29

◆　◆　◆

Model on Pattern Books,
Using Phonics for Writing
and Reading

Overview

These are the topics you will meet in this chapter:

- Predictable Stories
- Alphabet Patterns From Simple to Complex
- Patterns of Conversation in Predictable Stories
- Adding Phonics to Predictable Writing
- Other Pattern Books for Modeling

PREDICTABLE STORIES

You have been reading *predictable books*, that are also called *pattern books*, aloud to your pupils all year. In chapter 4, you learned about promoting participation at read-aloud time by having your pupils chime in on the predictable chants of the gingerbread man and the three little pigs. A child knows what's coming in a pattern story, and can recite parts of the text as a preliminary step to reading.

Such stories are useful also as models for writing. They give your pupils a pattern or guide for writing their own story. When your early learners made their first "1, 2, 3" books, they used counting books as their model. So they understand how to imitate a very simple pattern.

Alphabet Patterns From Simple to Complex

Alphabet books also provide patterns that are easy to imitate. For writing practice, your children can print matching capital and lower-case letters on 26 pages—A and a, B and b, through the whole alphabet. For phonics practice, they can paste pictures that begin with a on the first page, with b on the second page, and can try to spell the words that go with the pictures.

From this simplest pattern for an alphabet book, your pupils may progress to more complex patterns, such as the one in the book, A, My Name is Alice by J. Bayer (Dial). After your children have heard you read the book several times, you can introduce them to the game, perhaps with an altered pattern.

Remember the chanting game—"A, my name is Alice, and my cousin's name is Albert. We live in Alabama and we eat apples." Before you and your pupils start on an alphabet book in this pattern, you should have them chant their way through many rounds of the game where they come up with nouns of their own choosing.

The first few letters of the alphabet are relatively easy. "B, my name is Bernie, and my cousin's name is Belinda. We live in Brazil and we eat blueberries. C, my name is Carlee, and my cousin's name is Clifford. We live in Canada, and we eat cabbage." The end of the alphabet is not as easy. For the letter Z, Zach and Zelda of Zimbabwe can eat zucchini, but the letter X stumps most players.

When pupils model on the "A, my name is Alice" pattern or structure, they insert their own nouns to make the new book really their own. Your word wall would be a good resource for names of children and perhaps for names of foods, but you need maps and globes for place names.

Patterns of Conversation in Predictable Stories

Read-aloud books with predictable conversation patterns are good models for class books. Consider Marjorie Flack's predictable story, Ask Mr. Bear (Macmillan). In this story Danny wonders what to give his mother for her birthday. He decides to ask his friends, Mrs. Hen, Mrs. Goose, Mrs. Goat, Mrs. Sheep, and Mrs. Cow. He asks each one the same question: "Can you give me something for my mother's birthday?" Each animal suggests a gift, but in each case Danny replies that his mother already has whatever was suggested. Then he asks Mr. Bear and gets the best suggestion—a bear hug.

Danny's conversation with each animal follows the same question–answer pattern. Children can soon predict what he is going to say as he greets each animal.

Using the book Ask Mr. Bear as a model, one class wrote a story about getting a birthday present for dad, rather than mother. The children decided that in their version the story would take place in the city rather than on a farm. They even came up with a different ending, but still modeled on the conversation pattern of "Good morning, Mrs. ___ ," said Danny. "Can you give me something for my mother's birthday?" It provided the structure they needed.

Here is one class' predictable story containing the same pattern for each conversation:

> Danny wanted to give his dad a present for his birthday, so he went to the grocery store.
>
> "Good morning, Mr. Grocer," said Danny. "What can I give my dad for his birthday?"
>
> "You can give him spinach," said Mr. Grocer.
>
> "No, he doesn't like spinach," Danny said.
>
> Then he went to the candy store.
>
> "Good morning, Mr. Candyman," said Danny. "What can I give my dad for his birthday?"
>
> "You can give him chocolates," said Mr. Candyman.
>
> "No, he's on a diet," Danny said.
>
> Then he went to the toy store.
>
> "Good morning, Barbie," said Danny. "What can I give my dad for his birthday?"
>
> "You can give him clothes," said Barbie.
>
> "No, he has clothes," Danny said.
>
> Then he went to the pet store.
>
> "Good morning, Ms. Beagle," said Danny. "What can I give my dad for his birthday?"
>
> "You can give him a puppy," said Ms. Beagle. "I just had a litter of puppies, and I will give you one."
>
> "Thank you," Danny said. "My dad would like a puppy, and I would, too."

Adding Phonics to Predictable Writing

Consider the predictable folktale, *Chicken Little*. When a chestnut fell on Chicken Little's tail, she thought the sky was falling. So she told Ducky-Lucky, Goosey-Loosey, and Turkey-Lurkey. They joined her in getting upset. Each creature said, "Let's run and tell the king."

A teacher was working with a group of early writers who wanted to model on the structure of the *Chicken Little* story. But in their version, the ceiling (rather than the sky) was falling. They would run and tell the principal (rather than the king). And the names of the characters? They decided on Ginny-Linny, Mikey-Likey, and Rudy-Ludy. Clearly, they were modeling not only on the plot, but also on the rhyming names of the characters, as described here:

"How do you want to start your story?" the teacher asked her group of early writers.

"Once upon a time," Rudy volunteered quickly.

"Do we have any of those words on our word wall?" asked the teacher. "They are handy words to know. Lots of stories start with 'Once upon a time.'"

Mikey located the word *time* and the word *a* on the word wall.

"We still need the words *once* and *upon*," said Rudy.

"Here's how we spell *once*," said the teacher. "O - n - c - e. We use a capital O since the word starts a sentence. You can figure out the word *upon* with phonics. What sounds do you hear in *upon*?"

"Uh," said Ginny. "It's 'uh-pon.' I hear 'uh' at the beginning."

"What's the letter for that sound?" The teacher waited.

The children looked at the each other. Ginny kept saying, "Uh, uh, uh."

"A?" ventured Rudy.

Ginny shook her head. "No, not A. A doesn't say 'uh.' Listen: uh-pon."

"P," Mikey stated. "I hear the sound /p/ in the word *upon*."

"Wait," said the teacher. "You're getting ahead of yourself. There is a p in *upon*. You hear the sound /p/, but it is not the first sound. The letter u stands for the sound you made, Ginny, 'uh.' So the first two letters of upon are u and p. What do you think the last letter is? Uponnnnnn?"

This teacher demonstrated the usefulness of phonics for writing and spelling while she helped her pupils compose their version of the *Chicken Little* story.

OTHER PATTERN BOOKS FOR MODELING

Folktales like *The Three Bears* and *Little Red Riding Hood* have patterns that are easy to imitate. But many newer books also provide structures on which your pupils can model their stories. Perhaps some of these titles are in your library.

- Aardema, V. *Bringing the rain to Kapiti Plain*. Dial.
- Butler, J., & Schade, S. *I love you, good night*. Simon & Schuster.
- Emberley, B. *Drummer Hoff*. Prentice-Hall.
- Grossman, B. *My little sister ate one hare*. Crown.
- Hennessy, B. G. *The missing tarts*. Viking.
- Martin, B., & Carle, E. *Polar bear, polar bear, what do you hear?* Simon & Schuster.
- Neitzel, S. *The jacket I wear in the snow*. Greenwillow.
- Pilkey, D. *'Twas the night before Thanksgiving*. Orchard.
- Speed, T. *Two cool cows*. Scholastic.

Modeling on predictable patterns is a good strategy to use with early learners. They have a guide for their project, and can feel creative when writing their own new versions of old stories.

30

◆ ◆ ◆

Present High-Frequency Words in Age-Appropriate Ways

Overview

These are the topics you will meet in this chapter:

• Need for Recognition of High-Frequency Words
• Words That are Also Letters
• Phonics and Context for the Word "and"
• "The," the Most Frequently Used Word
• Time to Pause

NEED FOR RECOGNITION OF HIGH-FREQUENCY WORDS

Two of the most frequently used words in our language are also letters of the alphabet. They are the words *I* and *a*. The word *and* is our most frequently used conjunction. But the word at the top in all frequency counts is the word *the*.

In print, it is hard to find a paragraph, or even a sentence, that does not contain the word *the*. So your early readers need to develop instant recognition of this word. But the strategies you used for teaching the "when" and "where" words (chap. 27) will not work for an abstract word like *the*. You can not "strengthen the concept before presenting the word in print" because there is no concept connected with *the*.

Besides *the, and, I,* and *a,* there are many other high-frequency words that readers also need to recognize by sight. But beginners should tackle only a few at a time because they are hard to learn. You can provide oral–aural experiences with these words before you ask a child to read and write them, and that is some help. But they are still difficult.

Here are some developmentally appropriate strategies that you can use when you introduce your early learner to the four previously mentioned, high-frequency words.

Words That are Also Letters

The word *I* is a letter. So is the word *a.* Let's consider how you might teach the recognition of each of these words.

If your early reader knows the letter *I* by name, you can easily teach the word *I.* Point out that, when it is used as a word, *I* always appears as a capital letter. Encourage your pupil to use the word *I* orally by playing the "I spy" game.

That game can also provide oral practice on the word *a.* "I spy a pan. Where is it?" (On the play stove.) Or "I spy a word that starts with the sound /p/. Find it." (On the label of a can of pears.)

On your experience chart, you can set up many four-word sentences that contain the words *I* and *a,* such as:

- I see a cat.
- I want a pet.
- I have a dog.
- I ate a sandwich.
- I called a friend.

For some children, you can use words from their wordbanks so that they can read the sentences. For others, you can suggest taking turns. The child will read the first word and you will read the second. Then it is the child's turn again for the third word. This "taking turns" gives your pupil repeated practice at reading the words *I* and *a.*

Because the letter i is read as the word *I* only when it appears as a capital letter, you need to point out that the letter a "behaves" differently. The first letter of the alphabet, both as a capital letter and as a lower-case letter, stands for the word *a.* Write the sentence, "A dog chased a cat." Point out both the A at the beginning of the sentence and the a close to the end. Tell your early learner that both forms of the letter, A and a, stand for the word *a.* To have a pupil use the word orally, ask, "What are you wearing?" The child is very likely to use the word *a* in replying, "A sweater," or "A bracelet," or "A new belt." For further oral practice, you might say, "Name three things on my desk." Your pupil's answers might be, "A pencil, a stapler, and a book."

The words *I* and *a* appear frequently in the speech balloons of comic strips. You could have an early learner hunt for and mark them with a highlighter. When you and the child read the comic strip together, let your pupil read the marked words.

Phonics and Context for the Word "And"

The word *and* is phonetically regular, so it is easy to blend the sounds /a/, /n/, and /d/ into the word *and*. It is also easy to promote oral use of the word. Just ask a child, "What does your Mommy buy at the grocery store?" The answer will probably contain quite a few repetitions of the word *and*: "Bread and cheese and crackers and ... "

Any picture of two items can have a caption that includes the word *and*. Magazine ads feature girls and boys, shirts and pants, cups and saucers. You can encourage your early writers to make such captions for display with the pictures. When children add multiple copies of the wordcard *and* to their wordbanks, they can create long sentences, such as "Dogs and cats and boys and girls run."

The type of sentence used in teaching the words *I* and *a* can be expanded when your children recognize *and*. "I see a cat" can become "I see a cat and a dog."

"The," the Most Frequently Used Word

Do not expect instant success when you start to teach the word *the*. This word is hard for young children to "hang on to" because it does not have any meaning by itself. Because of its frequency, however, it is a word that you need to introduce before you start moving your early learners to independently reading easy library books.

After showing your child the word *the* on a wordcard, say:

> *This is the word the. Let's read it together: the.*
> *Now let's spell it together: t - h - e.*
> *At the beginning of a sentence,*
> *you write it with a capital T: The.*
> *Let's find this word on the page I'm reading.*

Read aloud to your pupil from any book. Stop and show your child the word *the* every time it appears. Let your pupil read *the* aloud each time you point to it.

When your early learner begins to recognize *the*, have the child hunt for it before you read a paragraph or a page, to see how very frequently it appears. But do not be surprised if the child mistakenly points out a number of words that look similar to *the*, such as *then, them, their, there*, and *these*. Some readers are well into the primary grades before they can discriminate quickly and accurately among all the *th* words.

As always, early reading and early writing go well together, so have your pupil trace and print *the* for further reinforcement. When your pupil starts printing the word *the* in his or her own stories, your teaching job on that word has reached successful completion.

TIME TO PAUSE

After teaching the high-frequency words *the, and, I,* and *a,* go back to easier words. Have your pupils come up with additional concrete nouns and verbs they would like to learn to read. Make sure they can read all the names of classmates from your word wall.

Is their recognition of the words *no* and *yes* firm? Or do they need more review? Can they read any words that answer the questions *where* and *when?* Even words that tell where and when are easier than abstract words like *the* for most early readers, so keep the ratio of difficult words low.

The learning of a few high-frequency words enables some early readers to start the transition from personalized books and class-written books to preprimers and easy-to-read storybooks for beginners. Of course, every commercially published book provides additional practice on high-frequency words because those words appear so often in written language. Your pupil's recognition of high-frequency words will be strengthened by whatever the child reads.

31

◆ ◆ ◆

Use the Library to Extend Reading, Writing, and Arithmetic

<table>
<tr><td>

Overview

These are the topics you will meet in this chapter:

• From Roots to Wings
• Success With an Easy-to-Read Library Book
• How the Librarian Can Help With Your Early 3 Rs Program

</td></tr>
</table>

FROM ROOTS TO WINGS

When you started your early 3 Rs program, you wrote a lot of individualized, personalized books for your children. No doubt you were their favorite author of stories they could actually read. Perhaps they loved the counting books you helped them make even more than the counting books from the library you read aloud to them. You have made sure that your early learners are firmly rooted in the basics of reading, writing, and arithmetic.

But now, thanks to your excellent teaching, some of your pupils can start to spread their wings as learners by independently reading easy library books. Here's how you can make sure an early learner will be successful at reading a book he or she has never seen before.

Success With an Easy-to-Read Library Book

In most of today's libraries you can find storybooks for beginners that are written in very limited vocabularies. Some libraries carry series of short, simple books that contain very few words. Check out the easiest library books you can find. See what ones contain words that are on your word wall, or are in the individual wordbanks of some of your early learners. List the words that a particular pupil needs to know in order to read the book independently.

You want your pupil to experience success on at least the first few pages, so don't let the child see the book until you are sure he or she can manage to read those pages independently. Using phonics and wordcard strategies, you can teach in advance most of the words that your pupil will meet in the easy book. So you can insure a successful experience.

Then it's safe to present the library book to your child and say, "You can read this one on your own." It's a milestone when a child first reads a book that he or she has never seen before.

This feat calls for a celebration!

A fitting celebration might be helping the child get that all-important first library card, and your librarian will be delighted to help.

How the Librarian Can Help With Your Early 3 Rs Program

Today's librarians often like to work in partnership with teachers. You may want to ask your librarian for help not only with getting early library cards for your children but also with providing these other services for your early 3 Rs program:

- Conducting library tours for early learners
- Finding books on topics of personal interest for each of your children
- Giving you early access to holiday books
- Setting aside special collections for you of alphabet books, counting books, concept books, wordless books, and classic favorites
- Providing you with enrichments to accompany some of the most popular children's books (audiotapes, book and cassette packages, videotapes, phonics kits, CD-ROMs, manipulatives)
- Doing puppet shows, read-alouds, or storytelling performances for your pupils
- Supplying recommended book lists to send home to parents for the children's holiday or summer reading

You may also want to ask about special check-out privileges, that often include keeping a large number of books for an extended period of time, in order to enrich your classroom library.

Young children who learn to love the library keep using it to help themselves progress in reading, writing, and arithmetic as they progress through school. When you make the library an integral part of your early 3 Rs program, you are giving your children roots and wings for lifelong learning.

32

♦ ♦ ♦

Summary of Unit IV

HOW TO SMOOTH THE TRANSITION
INTO 3 Rs IN THE PRIMARY GRADES

Transitional activities can help some early learners make further progress in reading, writing, and arithmetic, but are not suitable for every child. You need to decide which of your pupils can benefit from which approaches as you try these activities.

Strengthen *When* and *Where* Concepts
as Background for Print

Your children need to be clear on the concepts of words that tell *where*, and numbers as well as words that tell *when*. Only after these concepts are firm can your pupils start reading and writing prepositions, calendar words, and numbers.

Play Games That Require Early Arithmetic

Adaptations of some board games, card games, classic games, hiding–finding games, and measuring and estimating contests can help your early learners apply their math skills and move forward in arithmetic in a play situation. As you play these games with them, you move them toward the primary grades operations of mathematics.

Model on Pattern Books, Using Phonics
for Writing and Reading

When your pupils model on predictable stories, they get the structure they need for producing their own new versions of these books. As they compose interactively with you, you can lead them to use phonics to spell the words they want to write and read.

Present High-Frequency Words
in Age-Appropriate Ways

The words *the, and, I,* and *a* appear very frequently in print, so your early readers need to learn to recognize them. In teaching them, you can use strategies that are developmentally appropriate for your early 3 Rs program. Your children can move more easily into reading easy library books if they can recognize some high-frequency words.

Use the Library to Extend Reading, Writing, and Arithmetic

You can make a special occasion of your child's first experience of independently reading a library book . The child's success merits the acquisition of a library card. Your librarian can help with this endeavor, and may offer other services that are of value to your early 3 Rs program.

◆ ◆ ◆

Epilogue

Congratulations, teacher!

You have launched your pupil into early reading, writing, and arithmetic. But remember that the child still enjoys these activities most in partnership with *you*.

Keep reading aloud to your pupil, but sometimes, have the child read aloud to you. When the child reads silently, you'll want to discuss the material to insure good comprehension was achieved.

Now that your pupil can print, the child no longer needs you as scribe. But you are wanted and needed greatly as editor, correspondent, and sometimes, as co-author.

Continue to speak arithme-talk with your pupil. Much math is learned orally, so you need to keep the conversations going.

You—the teacher—are the one who makes the learning of the 3 Rs happen, and you are the one who makes it fun! By working with your pupil in your early 3 Rs program, you provide a great start on reading, writing, and arithmetic. This is a gift of lifelong value!

◆ ◆ ◆

For Further Reading

Adams, M. J., Foorman, B. R., Lundberg, I., & Beeler, T. (1998). *Phonemic awareness in young children.* Baltimore, MD: Paul H. Brookes.

Barchers, S. I. (1998). *Teaching reading from process to practice.* Belmont, CA: Wadsworth.

Beeler, T. (1993). *I can read! I can write!* Cypress, CA: Creative Teaching Press.

Braddon, K., Hall, N. J., & Taylor, D. (1993). *Math through children's literature.* Englewood, CO: Teacher Ideas Press.

Butler, D., & Clay, M. M. (1987). *Reading begins at home.* Portsmouth, NH: Heinemann.

Charlesworth, R. (1996). *Experiences in math for young children* (3rd ed.). Albany, NY: Delmar.

Crawley, S. J., & Mountain, L. (1995). *Strategies for guiding reading* (2nd ed.). Needham Heights, MA: Allyn & Bacon.

Cunningham, P. M., & Allington, R. L. (1999). *Classrooms that work: They can all read and write* (2nd ed.). New York: Longman/Addison Wesley.

Johnson, P. (1992). *A book of one's own: Developing literacy through making books.* Portsmouth, NH: Heinemann.

Kamii, C. (1982). *Number in preschool and kindergarten: Educational implications of Piaget's theory.* Washington, DC: National Association for the Education of Young Children.

Kennedy, M. M. (1998). *Learning to teach writing.* New York: Teachers College Press.

Leu, D. J. Jr., & Kinzer, C. K. (1999). *Effective literacy instruction, K–8* (4th ed.). Upper Saddle River, NJ: Merrill Prentice-Hall.

Lilburn, P., & Rawson, P. (1994). *Let's talk math.* Portsmouth, NH: Heinemann.

Marzano, R. J., & Paynter, D. E. (1996). *Literacy plus resource book.* Columbus, OH: Zaner-Bloser.

Mooney, M. E. (1990). *Reading to, with, and by children.* Katonah, NY: Richard C. Owen.

Morrow, L. M. (1989). *Literacy development in the early years.* Englewood Cliffs, NJ: Prentice-Hall.

Mountain, L. (1994). *Math detectives*. Austin, TX: Steck Vaughn/ Harcourt.

Mountain, L., Crawley, S. J., & Fry, E. (1994). *Pocketful of posies, teachers edition*. Providence, RI: Jamestown.

Paciorek, K. M., & Munro, J. H. (Eds.). (1998). *Early childhood education 98/99* (19th ed.). Guilford, CT: Dushkin/McGraw-Hill.

Polonsky, L., Freedman, D., Lesher, S., & Morrison, K. (1995). *Math for the very young: A handbook of activities for parents and teachers*. New York: Wiley.

Schiro, M. (1997). *Integrating children's literature and mathematics in the classroom*. New York: Teachers College Press.

Stewig, J. W., & Jett-Simpson, M. (1995). *Language arts in the early childhood classroom*. Belmont, CA: Wadsworth.

Thompson, B., & Nicholson, T. (Eds.). (1999). *Learning to read: Beyond phonics and whole language*. New York: Teachers College Press.

Wolfinger, D. M. (1994). *Science and mathematics in early childhood education*. New York: HarperCollins.

Index